T0328969

Title-page of the *Didactica Opera Omnia* of Comenius (Amsterdam, 1657)

THE TEACHER OF NATIONS

Addresses and Essays
in Commemoration of the visit to England of
the great Czech Educationalist
JAN AMOS KOMENSKÝ
COMENIUS
1641   1941

By
EDUARD BENEŠ
President of the Republic of Czechoslovakia

J. L. PATON	O. ODLOŽILÍK
HENRY MORRIS	OSKAR KOKOSCHKA
J. D. BERNAL, F.R.S.	DOROTHEA W. SINGER
R. FITZGIBBON YOUNG	J. G. CROWTHER
J. B. CONANT	ERNEST BARKER

Edited by
JOSEPH NEEDHAM
F.R.S.

With a Chronological Table
showing the events in the Life of Comenius
by R. FITZGIBBON YOUNG

and a Select Bibliography of the
Works of Comenius
by ANNA HEYBERGER
(translated by CORINNE BARHAM)

CAMBRIDGE
AT THE UNIVERSITY PRESS
1942

CAMBRIDGE
UNIVERSITY PRESS

University Printing House, Cambridge CB2 8BS, United Kingdom

Cambridge University Press is part of the University of Cambridge.

It furthers the University's mission by disseminating knowledge in the pursuit of education, learning and research at the highest international levels of excellence.

www.cambridge.org
Information on this title: www.cambridge.org/9781107511620

© Cambridge University Press 1942

First published 1942
First paperback edition 2015

A catalogue record for this publication is available from the British Library

ISBN 978-1-107-51162-0 Paperback

CONTENTS

UNIVERSITY OF CAMBRIDGE

Comenius Tercentenary Committee

THE VICE-CHANCELLOR.
H. BUTTERFIELD (Peterhouse), *Lecturer in History.*
SIR WILLIAM DAMPIER (Trinity College).
B. W. DOWNS (Christ's College), *Lecturer in English.*
G. HALOUN, *Professor of Chinese.*
JOSEPH NEEDHAM (Caius College), *Reader in Biochemistry.*
G. R. OWST (Emmanuel College), *Professor of Education.*

EDITORIAL INTRODUCTION

On Friday, 24 October 1941, the tercentenary of the visit to England in 1641 of Jan Amos Komenský (Comenius) was observed in the Senate House of the University of Cambridge, in the presence of official representatives of the governments of Czechoslovakia, the U.S.S.R., Poland, Yugoslavia, the Netherlands and Sweden, and of the Royal Society, the Board of Education, the Moravian Church, and the British Council, under the chairmanship of the Vice-Chancellor, Dr J. A. Venn of Queens' College. The Royal Society was represented by its President and three ex-Presidents, and the assembly included many eminent scholars and leaders of contemporary thought such as Mr H. G. Wells.

Addresses which were delivered by His Excellency Dr E. Beneš, President of the Republic of Czechoslovakia, by Mr J. L. Paton, by Professor J. D. Bernal, F.R.S. and by Professor Ernest Barker, will all be found in full in the present volume. They are accompanied by contributions from other scholars in honour of one of the greatest of Europeans. The title is taken from a phrase applied to Komenský by President Masaryk.

There is hardly any department of human experience in which we can feel reluctance in calling Komenský great. His influence was pre-eminent in religion, in science, in education, and in international politics. Komenský represented all the ideas which have successfully triumphed in modern education; he was in favour of the education of women, he was against class distinctions in the school, he wanted to introduce science, music and handwork at the expense of the Latin grammar which was at that time universally learnt by heart, he desired schools to be happy workshops of humanity (in his own words) rather than the torture-chambers of youth that they were. His basic belief was that man is a rational creature situated by God among visible creatures, the natures and properties of which he is necessitated to know. Hence the interest of Komenský in science ('the new or experimental philosophy') arose out of his interest in education, and that in turn sprang from his theoretical position as one of the great Christian humanists.

Like Browne, Komenský insisted that Christians ought to pay at least equal attention to that other bible, Nature, 'that open and publick manuscript which lies expans'd unto the eyes of all'. He had no fear that true religion and true science would ever conflict. Though Komenský made no scientific discoveries himself, he brought it about by his new ideas on education that men should arise who could make scientific discoveries. Like Boyle, Komenský combined a passionate belief in the growth of natural science with a universalism which desired the propagation of the Gospel in those far parts of the world with which the voyages of exploration had made Christians familiar. Like Boyle, Komenský was associated with New England. This Christian universalism was the mainspring of the interest of such men as Komenský and John Wilkins in a universal language, as well as in universally applicable methods of education, which should deal with things and actions, not with words and ideas. From the *Unitas Fratrum* (the Bohemian Brethren) came the ideas of *unitas* and *communitas* which dissolved the secrecy of the alchemists and astrologers into the more liquid homogeneity of a higher level of international collaboration in science, in religion, and in education. In Komenský we rightly commemorate the spiritual father of the Invisible College and the patron saint of all those who are conscious of the social relations and function of science.

The historical connexions between Science and Liberty have still to be fully worked out, but it is surely significant that Komenský, the prophet of science in the service of a universally conscious and rational humanity, connects in his own person and wanderings two foci of freedom in European history. The Bohemia from which he was fleeing had been the theatre of great defensive wars for freedom of religion for two centuries previously. The Hussites, as Professor Ernest Barker points out, had been the Ironsides of Central Europe; the Taborites had been its Levellers—for between religious and political concepts there was in those days no line of distinction. And the England to which Komenský was travelling was about to be the scene of the first and greatest triumph of that rising industrial class whose destiny it was to transform European civilization by the overthrow of feudalism. This triumph was the triumph of the Parliamentary armies in the English Civil War, and if in the process their most advanced groups were destroyed, if in the end a stable compromise was effected under the forms of monarchy, it was none the less a vast and permanent setting forward of the liberties of England. Thus the frustrated stirrings of fifteenth-century Bohemia and sixteenth-century Germany won their first decisive victory in seventeenth-century England and their second in eighteenth-century France. The moral for our own troubled day is obvious, but we may take heart from the example of Komenský, who, though in a small minority, laboured to convince; though an exile, never despaired of his native land; though a rational Christian in the midst of irrational tyrannies, never believed that they would be the final victors. May the time soon come when that commonwealth which neither fifteenth-century Bohemia nor seventeenth-century England could permanently retain, will unite all humanity as the waters cover the sea.

J. N.

CAIUS COLLEGE
CAMBRIDGE
31 DECEMBER 1941

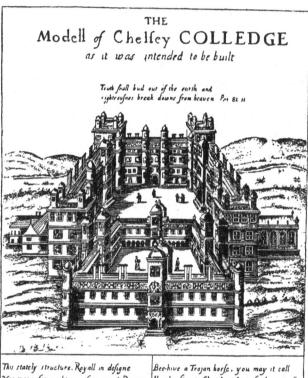

THE
Modell *of* Chelfey COLLEDGE
as it was intended to be built

Truth fhall bud out of the earth and
righteoufnes break downe from heaven P. 81 11

This stately structure. Royall in defigne	Bee-hive a Trojan horfe, you may it call
Yea more, for mighty reafons, most Divine	Heav'ns fire, to Church & State for happy wall
Wch Soviaigns Senats, Synods, wifedome too,	Hells hate, Romes horror, of our puyfon'd tymes
Did vote promote and fort, the Kingdome wooe	The best of Antidotes, to purge the erymes
Els not mahgnd foe Had it its end	Shal't finke ' O fhame' may't shine yet to Godi glory
Vowes Hirefyes to chooke, Truth to defend	And found the Parliaments æternall story .

Chelsea College was established as a theological seminary in 1609 by
James I and when Comenius visited England in 1641 plans were made
for converting it into a "Pansophic College" according to his design
(see pp. 5, 32, 51). But owing to the Civil War the project became as
visionary as Bacon's "Solomon's House" or Cowley's "Philosophicall
Colledge" and the organisation of science had to await the development
of the Invisible College into the Royal Society. In 1682 under Charles II
Chelsea College became the well-known Military Pensioners' Hospital.

The Place of Comenius in History as a Good European

By EDUARD BENEŠ

President of the Republic of Czechoslovakia

It is with real delight that I find myself with you again to-day in your old University town of Cambridge for the purpose of commemorating the life and activity of that great world citizen of the seventeenth century, John Amos Comenius. This great Czech patriot and one of the most famous sons of the Czechoslovak people, who left his country on the eve of the extinction of its independence in 1628 and travelled for more than forty years across the whole of Europe, working without rest for the salvation of his nation, as well as for his scientific and educational plans, is deeply venerated by all Czechoslovaks, particularly now, when a similar fate has overtaken us and we are fighting for the same lofty human ideals and moral values for which he fought three centuries ago.

He was born in Komna[1] in Moravia in 1592 and died in Amsterdam in 1670. It was at a time when, as a result of the religious conflicts of the seventeenth century and the Thirty Years' War, his country had to undergo great tribulations. These began with the defeat of the Czechs at the battle of the White Mountain in 1620, the first great engagement of the war. Komenský lived through his nation's humiliation in all its fullness, and throughout the whole of his life in exile fought against the German Empire, then under the Hapsburgs, for the liberation of his country from the subjugation which resulted from this battle. In his well-known prophecy, which became our watchword in the last war as well as in the present one, he announced the renaissance of his people, when he declared: 'I too believe before God that when the storms of wrath have passed, to thee shall return the rule over thine own things, O Czech people!'

And after a struggle lasting for three hundred years this liberation was finally achieved in 1918, under the leadership of another great Czechoslovak, and a follower of Komenský, President

---

[1] See footnote on p. 86.

Masaryk. But after a happy existence for twenty years another criminal attack was made upon our people in 1938 by Hitler's Germany. And it is natural that our present struggle should be conducted once more in the name of these two great Czechoslovaks, both of whom were born in the same region lying between the Czechs and the Slovaks: Komenský and Masaryk.

The Czechs are not naturally inclined to war. They yearn instinctively for peace, for hard and steady work in quietness and calm. But they are firm, consistent, enduring and stubborn, obstinate in a struggle, not disposed to give way, and in *this* sense, very combative. But they wish for peace both for themselves and for others. If we study Czech history we meet with this trait in their character at every step.

At the time when Komenský was alive, the conflict between Catholicism and Protestantism divided the Czech people—like most of the European peoples—into two camps, the majority being on the side of the Protestants. The German and Hapsburg victory of the White Mountain led to the Counter-Reformation; everywhere in the country Catholicism was introduced by force, and the political independence of Bohemia began to decay under the new and absolute constitution of 1627. Unyielding, and firm in their faith, the evangelicals and the Brethren, the most prosperous and educated elements in the population, the real flower of the Czech people, were obliged to leave their country.

Amongst these Czechs who had been driven abroad by the Hapsburgs was Komenský. He spent more than forty years of his life in unhappy exile. Although he was a great 'citizen of the world' he remained always a great Czech patriot.

The path of his life was originally to have been that of the teacher and the theologian. It was from this point of view that he began his work as a young student at the German University in Heidelberg. While still a youth he was versed in all the science and philosophy of the Bible, and even went so far as to plan an encyclopaedia of science and human knowledge. He described it as a Pansophia, and worked upon the project the whole of his life.

Taking his departure from this fundamental standpoint, he then devoted his attention to the question of popular and general education. And along these lines he developed into one of the first and the greatest of modern educationalists. He was such both in practice, as a teacher and professor in a number of schools, and also in theory, as the author of a series of books on education and educational manuals, and through having been invited to a number of states in order to organize therein popular and school education. He was very industrious; he wrote more than ninety religious, educational and political works, all with a broad and universal outlook. He was certainly amongst the greatest and most enlightened spirits of his time, and is rightly described as one of the first modern educators—a teacher of the nations.

He was also a theologian, an interpreter of the Bible, and finally a bishop of the Church of the Bohemian Brethren. He was religious to the point of being mystical, and took a part, both conciliatory and controversial, in the struggles between the Catholic and the Protestant world at the time of the Thirty Years' War in Bohemia and elsewhere. This took him into the field of practical politics, in which as a teacher and a bishop he remained until his death.

In his stormy life as a teacher, an educator, a bishop and a politician in exile he travelled over almost the whole of Europe. Permit me to devote a few words to his journey to England, as in recalling his name to-day, we recall also before everything his relation to this country, in which three hundred years ago he received hospitality at the time when his own country was stricken; and as an exile, just as we are to-day.

Komenský left for England in September 1641. At this time the economic and moral consequences of the Thirty Years' War had assumed the most terrible forms. It was impossible to say when the war would end; practically the whole of Europe was gradually being drawn into it. The fate and the further development of the civilized world were at stake. And then also it was England before everybody else which was striving for peace and religious freedom.

In Komenský's programme for world work two main objects were emphasized: The need to unite as soon as possible all the Christian churches on the basis of Protestantism, and thus to create *a religious peace*; and in the second place to carry out reforms in the field of education and scientific research which would make it possible to raise the cultural level of different nations to such a degree that the ground could be prepared for *permanent political peace.*

The basis of the so-called pansophic studies of Komenský was the principle that all created things have an interior association between them, that they are logically connected with one another, and that all of them can be accommodated in a common system of knowledge. The same logical harmony should exist between all the creatures in the world. Just as human knowledge is split up, and divided into smaller and smaller elements which are often mutually contradictory, so according to Komenský are the different nations chaotically divided without any will to unity, harmony and peace. Hence it is necessary first of all to unify all human knowledge and science into one harmonious system which will ultimately lead to a general harmony on the human plane, and to collaboration between nations, which would provide a means for escaping from their everlasting mutual difficulties.

According to the plans of Komenský and his friends the services of a number of other learned men were to be secured, who in the spirit of his teachings were to work out certain sections of his pansophic scientific system. Komenský himself was to elaborate the general principles involved and his collaborators were to develop them scientifically. The most suitable retreat for undertaking such labour in this disturbed period, in the opinion of Komenský, was England.

A year before Komenský reached England, on 3 November 1640, the Long Parliament met. On the instigation of Samuel Hartlib, a devoted friend and follower of Komenský in England, John Gauden, later Bishop of Exeter and Worcester, introduced into his speech on 'The love of truth and peace' before the assembled Parliament, cordial references to Jan Komenský and John Durie, calling the attention of those present to their labours in the field of education and the unification of the churches. This address made a considerable stir in the House.

On the invitation of Hartlib Komenský proceeded to England, entered into important contacts with the political and scientific world, and developed his whole plan. It seemed that his dream was to be realized. A special commission was to be established in Parliament to examine Komenský's projects. The idea of creating a special scientific college, which under Komenský's leadership would work out a pansophic system and place human education on a new and universal basis, either in Winchester College or the Savoy Hospital (Sabaudeum) in London, or finally in Chelsea, was taken into consideration.

With this great work of reforming educational methods and creating international peace leagues there was to be associated the selection of men from all over the world who would be in constant association with one another, and who would bring into being an international society for the realization of the whole plan. The centre was to be in London. The aim was to be throughout the same; to unite the whole of human knowledge into a system, to unite all the Protestant churches, to attain thereby to a religious peace, and on the foundation of both these things to create a society of nations and permanent political peace.

But even in England new political disturbances rendered the plan nugatory. At the beginning of November 1641 an insurrection broke out in Ireland; early in December the Grand Remonstrance was presented by Parliament to the King, and civil war began to loom ahead. Conditions continued to deteriorate, and all hopes for the college collapsed. With a heavy heart Komenský took his departure from this hospitable land, having left behind him there his complete work, 'Via lucis', in which he sketched out in full his political, scientific and educational programme.

The Peace of Westphalia of 1648, by which the Thirty Years' War was brought to an end, was for Komenský a cruel blow: the Hapsburgs remained German Emperors, and the Catholic Germans under their leadership won the war in the greater part of Germany and in the whole of the Hapsburg Empire. As a consequence the Czechs were completely overpowered and subjugated. The Kingdom of Bohemia fell, the Czech protestants were unable to return home, and Komenský became definitely outlawed. He lost his fatherland.

But even this blow did not discourage him in his projects. In his book, 'Panegersia', published at that time, he states:

We are all fellow-citizens of one world, all of one blood, all of us human beings. Who shall prevent us from uniting in one republic? Before our eyes there is only one aim: the good of humanity, and we will put aside all considerations of self, of nationality and sectarianism.

Komenský turned again to the conception of world peace in 1667, when he published his 'Angel of Peace', which was sent by him to the English and Dutch ambassadors in Breda who were at the time negotiating regarding peace between their two countries. But it was addressed also to all the nations of the world 'to persuade them to abandon war and to create instead the Kingdom of Peace, of Christ, who wishes only to declare peace to the nations'.

Here Komenský is expressly calling for religious and political tolerance between all nations. Thus he says quite unambiguously:

We must take measures to prevent the evils which have crept in through the abuse of God's power; Christians must agree in a brotherly fashion as to which nations shall have the most right to sail the seas, with what object and under what conditions. Certainly all those who live near the ocean will claim such rights. But some general scheme would be needed so that their interests did not clash.

And in another place he declares:

And you, ambassadors of peace, that you may live up to your name, do not only consider human, but also divine, plans; take account not only of what is asked of you by your kings, but also what is asked of you by the King of Kings; let your aim be, not war, but peace. Do not write your agreements and treaties only on parchment, but also on your hearts; do not confirm them only with silver seals but also with the great name of God; do not take oaths in deceptive human language, but from the depths of the soul, which is witnessed and searched by God in virtue of that truth which is in Christ.

Through his demands for peace courts, for international consultations and the unified direction of human affairs he caused a commotion in Europe. Komenský had a premonitory apprehension of peace ideals far beyond his time; through his universal genius he had a European and a world consciousness even in the first half of the seventeenth century. In spite of his burning Czech patriotism he was always a good European and a man whose sympathies were world-embracing.

I will now bring to a close this short sketch of Komenský's political activities.

He is a typical Czech patriot. Since the tenth century the Czechoslovak nation has been surrounded by superior numbers of German tribes and peoples and has been obliged to fight for its national and state existence. Its territory is really the heart of Europe. It lies geographically at the cross-roads of three cultures, to the north the German, to the east the Slavonic and to the west the Latin. Hence the Bohemian lands are, and have always been, like Belgium and Holland, key positions in Europe. Bismarck was justified in declaring that he who was the ruler of Bohemia was the ruler of Europe. To gain possession of this area is to acquire an open door to the east against the Poles and the Russians, and to the south towards the Balkans and the Mediterranean, which means the domination of the whole of Central and South-Eastern Europe. It is for this reason that the Munich Agreement, which handed Czechoslovakia over to Germany, was a momentous mistake both for Europe and the world.

But it is for this reason also that every Czechoslovak, if he is politically educated, thinks in European and not only in Czechoslovak terms. Throughout all Czech history and culture a feeling for Bohemia has always been associated with a feeling for Europe and for humanity in general. We Czechoslovaks are conscious of the fact that we are a small nation in the heart of Europe, that geographically we are constricted by our environment, that we have round us large and powerful nations, who have been oppressing us and devouring our national substance for the last ten centuries, and that our strength cannot therefore be only material and our defence only physical and military.

Our future lies in moral strength, in spiritual maturity and education, in the power deriving from the unity of the nation, in liberty and peace, defended in co-operation with all men of good will in the rest of Europe. Hence we Czechoslovaks are and have always been essentially Europeans. As a consequence we are for peace, we were for the League of Nations, for freedom, for democracy, for religious and moral progress.

And for this reason also we are and have been always the most politically, economically and morally progressive of all the Central European nations in respect of individual freedom.

It is on this account that in the fifteenth century we had the great national philosopher, Peter Chelčický, who four centuries before Tolstoi gave expression to his ideas regarding universal peace, self-sacrifice and the religious life of the individual and the nation; that at the beginning of the fifteenth century we had John Hus, who a hundred years before Luther raised his voice in the cause of national freedom and religious reform, not only for his people and his own political cause—which was the principle by which Luther was guided—but for freedom, religious life and social and political justice for the whole of Europe and the world.

For this reason also we had the so-called Hussite King Jiří (George) of Poděbrady in the second half of the fifteenth century, who promulgated, and defended with his armies, religious freedom, effected a peaceful reconciliation between the Catholics and the Protestants of his country, and finally proposed to the Pope the institution of a League of Nations for the defence of peace and Christian Western European civilization.

Hence also the fact that in the Thirty Years' War our representative and spokesman was Komenský, a European, a precursor of those who were seeking for peace and religious freedom in the nineteenth and twentieth centuries.

The whole modern Czech generation of politicians, philosophers and scientific workers in the eighteenth and nineteenth centuries followed these Czech national leaders. Thomas Masaryk at the end of the nineteenth century and in the last war, and I myself in all my political work from the last war to the present one, both consciously and deliberately drew our inspiration from our great predecessors.

Such is the great and momentous difference which in politics stands forth to-day between ourselves and the Germans—a difference expressed in the names of Bismarck and Hitler on the one hand and of Komenský and Masaryk on the other.

Three centuries ago the whole fight for peace and religious freedom started in Bohemia through the conflict between the Czechs and the German Emperors. In 1648 at the Peace of Westphalia, when Komenský was desperately fighting for the freedom of his country, we were abandoned by Europe, just as we were in 1938. The present European war began in 1938 by the attacks of the German dictator against Czechoslovakia. But in the present struggle we are not, and I am sure we shall not be, deserted. The year 1938 foreshadowed clearly the terrible fate which was to fall upon all the peoples of Europe which are now subjugated, and all the dangers which threatened them. To-day we are fighting Nazism in allied unity with the help of British democracy, the great free republic of America and the valiantly resisting armies and people of the Soviet Union. And we shall this time preserve at any price the ideals of freedom and peace which were first, three hundred years ago, held up before the world by Jan Amos Comenius.

In accordance with Comenius' prophecy, his country will emerge again from the present war free, and the direction of their own national affairs will again be in the hands of the Czechoslovak people.

Comenius as a Pioneer of Education

By J. L. PATON

*formerly High Master of Manchester Grammar School and
President of University College, Newfoundland*

It is to Czech students at Oxford we owe it that Wyclif's books found their way to the University of Prague and John Hus was stirred in reading them into revolt against the corruptions of the mediaeval Latin Church. With the followers of Hus and Peter Chelcický began the Unitas Fratrum or Bohemian Brothers who chose Comenius as bishop.

It was two Czech students at Cambridge who spoke to Samuel Hartlib, Milton's friend, telling him of the great work Comenius was doing to reform the schools on the continent. One of these two had served Comenius as secretary.

'What doth he then at present, seeing that he hath published his "Janua Linguarum"?' 'He is writing a "Janua Rerum".' 'And what might that be?' asked Hartlib. 'By another name it might be called "Christian Pansophy", inasmuch as it sets forth the distributions and true definitions of all things.'

And so it came about that Hartlib began to correspond with Comenius and eventually brought him over to London three hundred years ago.

First of all, it will be well to get our great bishop into the right context as an educator. Educators have been of two orders—firstly, those who have been school teachers, practitioners of the art; secondly, those who have written wisely and effectually about education but have not been themselves teachers. Comenius was both practitioner and thinker. Also, his textbooks and treatises number well nigh a hundred. Over half the schools of Europe used his textbooks, which were translated into some seventeen languages. How could he possibly have done all this for teaching and at the same time have fulfilled his duties as bishop? There was no sense of inconsistency in Comenius' own mind. His ordination vow drew no line of distinction between two kinds of knowledge, religious and profane. Both were knowledge of God. It is as much the Christian's duty to add to his faith knowledge, as to add to his faith virtue. To know more of God's creation is to increase in love of the Creator. Our love is in direct ratio to our knowledge. Knowledge is an integral part of personal salvation; it is bound up also in the social salvation of the community. The salvation of the community could not be accomplished until the great breach in Christendom was healed. Comenius held that the cause of this great breach and of its continuance was precisely lack of knowledge. With fuller knowledge on both sides he prayed that the way of reunion might still be found.

That things were all wrong with the schools in the seventeenth century was only too obvious to all men who could see and think. Schoolboys knew it feelingly. It was Comenius' own experience of that wrongness that made him work so long and so laboriously for their reform. It was not till the age of sixteen that he himself had his first taste of school. It was a bitter taste—so bitter that, young as he was, he made up his boyish mind to do all in his power, when he came to man's estate, to find out some better way.

When a boy entered the Latin school, he was pitchforked at once into learning by heart the Latin Grammar. This was written in Latin and was quite unintelligible to him. It contained all the declensions, conjugations, prepositions and their cases, the gender rules with long lists of exceptions, the rules of syntax, etc. Boys were kept at it day by day, eight hours a day, for six years and sometimes as many as ten years. And after all this portentous waste of time they could neither speak Latin, nor understand Latin, nor even read Latin. As Comenius pointed out, a camp follower or scullion, moving about with the troops, would in three years learn how to carry on a conversation in two or three new languages. This Latin business was drummed into the boys with the cane or birch. The schools were, in Comenius' phrase, 'not workshops of humanity but torture houses'.

And all this inhumanity was perpetrated in the name (save the mark) of 'humanitas'. It bred in the boys—it could not help but breed—an ineradicable detestation of the process of education and all that belonged to it. Along these lines there was no 'advancement' of learning.

Wherever Comenius could hear of others like-minded with

himself, he strove to get in touch with them. The most likely man he could hear of was Ratke (Ratich) of Holstein. He was twenty years older and had been speaking with great effect at Giessen and other German Universities on the better way in education. Ratke found a patron who had fitted out for him on the most liberal scale a new school at Koethen. He had engaged also a staff of teachers for Ratke to train on the new lines. Unfortunately, the whole scheme collapsed; in fact it never got started. The reason was Ratke's own personality. He was difficile—so difficile that he could not find a *modus vivendi* with his own staff. Also, he regarded his ideas as his own special patent. Unless he was paid in advance, he refused to share them. He had 'an eye on the main chance'. That was more important than any reform of the schools. Like Shelley he was beautiful but ineffectual—and no angel either. Comenius was thrown back on his own resources.

While waiting for the age at which he could be ordained, Comenius was already teaching. When ordained, he found himself at Fulnek in charge not only of the church but the school. From the outset he set himself here to do two things: (1) to think out the whole educational system afresh from the very beginning, (2) to think out side by side with this the foundation principles of the science of education, and the methods of teaching. He was the first to do this. He calls this treatise, 'The Great Didactic'. He starts with a definition: 'Man is so situated among visible creatures as to be (i) a rational creature, (ii) the lord of all creatures, (iii) a creature who is the image and joy of his Creator.' That is to say, he defines his educand in terms of what his Creator means him to become. The child's education is to help him to rise to the full title of his dignity. Modern authorities define man not in terms of what he is to be, but in terms of his antecedents. Education is, they say, to adapt man to his environment, by which they mean to make him become a sort of Mowgli, to drag him down, in fact, to the very environment out of which he has with endless struggles risen towards the light. Not an inspiring ideal. I am not discussing this—I am only suggesting that Comenius has some inspiration for us at the very opening of his great book on the science of education. There are seeds of knowledge, of virtue, of godliness implanted in us. These are the qualities which differentiate man from the lower members of creation. It is the educator's function to foster the growth of these seeds. Draw them out and you 'set free the imprisoned splendour of the soul'. If, on the other hand, you had asked the old-fashioned teachers for their definition of the boy, they would have said at once, 'He is full of original sin, rightly designated by his nurse as "a limb". He is cram-full of obduracy and therefore refuses to learn. He is so stupid that he cannot learn. All we can do, therefore, is to whip the offending Adam out of him.'

It is well to have this contrast clearly set out. The antagonism is irreconcilable. Comenius' new ideal represents not a mere reform but a fundamental revolution.

His whole philosophy of education is based on this. And for his method he goes to Nature and watches her at work. There was no psychology in those days. He reasons by analogy of both Nature and the Arts. It is not strictly logical. But for all that we have not yet outgrown the 'Great Didactic'.

His planning of education as a whole I must treat briefly. The first education of the young was left as a rule to the mother of the parish clerk. Comenius does not oust the mother. He starts education at birth. When you read his 'schola infantiae', his carefully thought out plan for the first six years of life, it is hard to believe that it was written more than a hundred years before Pestalozzi was born. In those first as yet unconscious days nothing is without significance—the mother's voice, her smile, her patience —all influence the child's fundamental attitude to life. 'By the tales told at their mother's knee do men live or die.' It is the early environment that counts. We must take all pains to make earliest education attractive. The titles of his books for the little ones, the 'Violarium' and the 'Rosarium', suggest the flowers our children love most. Let them from the first learn to regard a book as a source of pleasure.

There follows the Vernacular School, from six to twelve. All the teaching was done in the mother tongue. The prevalent custom had been hitherto to keep the primary school for girls—it was all they got—and such boys as were going to earn their living by the sweat of their brow. Those aiming higher went straight into the Latin School. Comenius claimed that all children without exception should attend the full six years of the Vernacular School. He drew up the syllabus of the whole course in detail; he provided textbooks, time-table, not forgetting games, singing, and the training of the hand.

Luther also was for all children to attend this school but was content with two hours a day in the case of labouring folk. Comenius makes no such exception. He was clear the girls should have education in the same measure as boys. The passage in which he urges this is Comenius at his best:

Nor can any reason be given why the other sex [note he does not say the *weaker* sex, as his translator makes him say] should be wholly shut out from liberal studies, whether in the native tongue or in Latin. For equally are they God's image: equally are they partakers of grace and of the Kingdom to come: equally are they furnished with minds agile and capable of wisdom, yea, often beyond our sex: equally to them is there a possibility of attaining high distinction, inasmuch as they have often been employed by God Himself for the government of peoples, the bestowing of wholesome counsels on Kings and Princes, the science of medicine and other things useful to the human race, nay, even to the prophetical office and the rattling reprimands of priests and bishops. [Evidently the fame of Jeannie Geddes had found its way overseas.] Why then should we admit them to the Alphabet, but afterwards debar them from Books? Do we fear their rashness? The more we occupy their thoughts, the less will there be in them for rashness, which springs generally from vacuity of mind.

This is the voice not of sentiment but of real chivalry.

All are to attend the Vernacular School. Church and State are to see to this. He stresses the word 'all'. 'It is undesirable', he says, 'to create distinctions either of sex or class, or to give some children grounds for considering their own lot with satisfaction and that of the others with scorn.' He had no use for snobbery. He was the first great democrat among educational thinkers.

Nor does he forget, when he stresses the word 'all', that there are children who are real dunderheads. 'How do you propose', says our American friend, 'to put a 5000-dollar education into a 5-cent boy?' Obviously his need of education is greatest of all. Comenius tells us the story of the unmanageable steed Bucephalus, and says, 'Alexander knew how to manage the unmanageable steed', which is true enough, but not much help to a teacher who is not of the Alexander breed.

The second main point is that Comenius is the first great Realist in education. He would have children of this Vernacular School stage taught by things they can see, touch, handle, smell. Children must study their immediate surroundings, sun, moon, stars, hills, valleys, streams, how men earn their living and manage their communal life, the management of the home, their own bodies, the cultivation of fields. They are taught to use their voices and their hands. They are encouraged to play. The educator notes how in games their whole personality is keyed up to forceful action. Humour, drama, imagination, all play their part.

The Latin School comes next, from twelve to eighteen years. He will not have this school reserved for the sons of the well-to-do, 'as though these were the only boys able to fill the same positions as their fathers'. In his school he provided a free table for poorer boys and other help as well. Had he not been poor himself?

Hitherto Latin had practically monopolized instruction at this stage; it absorbed eight hours a day. By his new method and his new textbooks, the 'Janua linguarum', the 'Janua rerum', the 'Orbis pictus', he manages to teach in a two-year course in two hours a day all the Latin they need to read—not Roman literature, but the Latin of the new literature of science.

Comenius, as the first great realist in education, acclaimed Bacon's 'Instauratio Magna'—it was to him the philosophy for which he had been waiting. His contemporaries were still learning their natural history from Aristotle, Ælian, Pliny the Elder. If, for instance, a question arose as to how many legs a caterpillar has, they would settle the argument not by catching a caterpillar but by seeing what the great authorities said on the point. 'Do not we ourselves dwell in the garden of Nature as well as the Ancients?' says Comenius. 'Why should not we use our eyes, ears and noses as well as they? Why should we need other teachers than these our own senses? Why should not we, instead of these dead books, lay open the living book of Nature?'

Let the children have direct experience of the things of Nature. Let them touch, feel, see, hear, get to know all they can, and then experiment for themselves, draw the object, and measure it for themselves. Then you are working along the lines of the children's own natural impulse. You are training them to take part in man's great war against ignorance, and to add to the sum of human knowledge.

Where do the Classical authors come in? They do not come in at all. They have had the monopoly for centuries. Now with the new knowledge that is crowding in upon mankind, we must bow them out. We cannot any longer encumber the curriculum. If they have any contribution to make in terms of human knowledge, let us have compendiums made and use those.

Worst of all, the Classics were pagan authors—their influence is demoralizing. They take us into lascivious society, to brothels and places of shame. Comenius quoted the authority of Christian Fathers in support of this view. The only exceptions he would allow were Plato, Epictetus and Seneca.

There were many who were afraid that this new Science men were gaining from the 'interrogation of Nature' would clash with Revelation. Comenius welcomed it with open arms as itself a new revelation. Contrary to tradition it was, but 'Christ called himself not Tradition but Truth'. If He and His message are truth, then every increase of knowledge can be used to enrich the truth that rests on Him. Comenius' break with the classical tradition was complete. This in itself accounts for Milton's adverse reaction to his system. The school is to be 'Pansophic', a centre from which the major Pansophia should broaden out in concentric circles with the growth of each new discovery.

Comenius put the art of teaching 'on the way of reaching such perfection that there should be as much difference between the old system and the new as between the old system of multiplying books by the pen and the new method of the printing press'. His aim was to multiply learned men as the press multiplies books which are the vehicles of learning. 'The multitude of the wise is the wisdom of the world.'

Hallam dismisses Comenius as a man who invented a new way

of teaching Latin. A really great historian should know how to recognize greatness when he sees it.

Comenius united greatness of heart and greatness of character to greatness of intellect. He was to the school children what Lord Shaftesbury was to the factory children—he abolished cruelty. He abolished the conditions which produced that cruelty—the inhuman taskwork. He brought the home into partnership with the teacher in the task of education. He installed the despised mother tongue into its due place as the vehicle of all primary instruction. He enriched the primary curriculum with the beginnings of geography, history, the economics and civics of daily life, with training of voice and hand, the habitudes of moral conduct and worship. He brightened their books and their classrooms with pictures and models, with cheerfulness and encouragement. Latin, which had been the bugbear of boyhood, he made the vehicle of such knowledge of the world we live in as would equip both boyhood and girlhood to take an intelligent share in that great Advancement of Science of which Francis Bacon was the pioneer.

One thing above all was needed to carry out his great plan and translate it into reality. It was an army of teachers, seized by his great vision and ready to throw themselves into the great task. Here is his appeal. If there ever was a man entitled to make such an appeal, it was he.

Do you also, instructors of the young, whose task it is to plant and water the tender grafts of paradise, pray with all earnestness that these aids to your labours [i.e. National Schools] may be perfected and brought into daily use as soon as possible. For since you have been called that 'you may plant the heavens and lay the foundations of the earth', what can be more pleasing to you than to reap as rich a harvest as possible from your labour? Therefore, let your heavenly calling, and the confidence of the parents who entrust their offspring to you, be as a fire within you, and give you and those who come under your influence no rest until the whole of your native land is lit up by this flaming torch.

Education and the Community[1]

By HENRY MORRIS
Director of Education for the County of Cambridgeshire

The educational principles established by the great' Czech in homage to whom this volume appears, have to-day been generally accepted in all the free countries of the world. There is therefore room for some consideration of the means whereby they may be actually incarnated in the developing civilization of both town and country.

'Each age is a dream that is dying and one that is coming to birth.' The English village as a social unit is a relic of the middle ages and the pre-industrial age of Comenius' own time, the seventeenth century. It belongs to a culture when there were no roads in the modern sense and no rapid transport, and when, from the point of view of industry and social services, it did not matter whether people lived in groups of two hundred, five hundred or a thousand. The economical provision of social services and amenities demands a social unit of many thousands; and this is the reason why not only the instrumental services, such as sanitation, water and light, but also the immense development of education, especially of the secondary and technical type during the nineteenth century, have taken place wholly in the *towns* of England. During the past thirty years, and even to-day, the countryside, if it desires educational opportunity, must seek it in the town. Since the industrial age began over a hundred years ago, the countryside, not only culturally and socially, but in economic opportunity, has been increasingly dependent on our urban civilization. Modern motor transport, rapid, cheap, and ubiquitous, is finally completing the process, so that the rural community of all ages, and especially the young, have their faces turned habitually to the town.

I suggest that we should be more realistic and less romantic about the village. The village has ceased to be an independent

---

[1] The substance of a paper read to the Education Section of the British Association, Blackpool, 1937.

social unit. It has its own psychological limitations:

> Below me, there, is the village, and looks how quiet and small
> And yet bubbles o'er like a city with gossip, scandal and spite,
> And Jack on his ale-house bench has as many lies as a Czar.

The history of civilization, it has been said, is the history of progressive towns dragging in their wake a reluctant countryside. The village looked at from the Tudor manor house or the Queen Anne rectory or the week-end cottage has quite a different aspect from that of the village worker and the village youth. By itself the independent village cannot provide that cultural and social fuller life which increased leisure and facilities make possible and which the young are determined to have. One of the most disastrous of our social failures is the omission, in spite of our enormous wealth, to provide on a wide and imaginative scale communal facilities for every kind of cultural and recreational pursuit. Our towns are squalid and chaotic dormitories sicklied o'er with commercialized amusement; they should be and one day will be deliberately organized by the community for the art of living the full life. Is it possible for the countryside to realize this ideal independently of the towns? That is the problem. The independent village has gone for ever. The only alternative to the complete subordination of the countryside to the town is the adoption of the *rural region* as a cultural and social unit, parallel to that of the town. The choice is no longer between village and town but between the rural region and the town. Unless we can interpose the rural region between the village and the town, the village is doomed and the victory of the town will be complete. I commend this to the consideration of those who imagine that they will preserve the village by resisting reorganization in rural education.

The modern transport that will otherwise transform our countryside into a vast and far-spread suburb can here be our friend—it can make the rural region compact and accessible from all points, and can weld it into a genuine social unity. Indeed, one type of rural region, namely the small country town of two or three thousand people and its adjacent villages, already exists as a traditional and geographical unit in the English countryside—transport will serve to reinforce it. The other kind of rural region, a group of villages centring round a large village, can, I suggest, be made into a no less successful cultural and social unit.

The Hadow report has been published for over ten years; and educationalists, administrators and the public are just becoming accustomed to the idea of Senior Schools in central places for the education of the older children of the countryside. For many years I have emphasized the need for providing the countryside with something much more comprehensive—that is, not only with a post-primary system for the older children but also for the fullest opportunities for adult education (including the countryside's own technical education in agriculture) and for recreation; that is, there should be a cultural and social life for the countryside in its own right and independent of that of the towns.

To achieve this the rural senior school as such in its strictly conventional conception, with limited buildings and accommodation, and with its peculiar adolescent ethos, is insufficient; it may, in fact, actually prove an obstacle, organize it as a 'night school' as much as we may. We must start with the conception of a community centre serving the population of a rural region at all points and at all ages—a community centre on as generous a scale as possible which, while housing the senior school in the day-time, will provide a theatre for the habituation of the adult community beyond the school-leaving age in Science and the Humanities and in health and the corporate life. We have been hearing much during the past two years about the development of technical and adult education and of physical training and health education. We cannot provide technical institutes for small country towns, much less for groups of villages. The only way in which technical and adult education can be shared by the country towns and villages of England is by means of the community centre which houses the senior school in the day-time. Here we have a solution that is at once effective and economical.

By means of such a rural community centre the wide provisions of the Education Act of 1921 (now supplemented by the Physical Training and Recreation Act of 1937), as they affect not only the school but higher and technical education, and social and recreational life, could be expressed with striking significance in terms of the life and industry of the countryside.

I turn to the physical embodiment of the rural community centre of the countryside, that is to its buildings. Parenthetically, I should like to express the wish that we would allow our young architects to design our new schools. The architectural intelligence of England is for all practical purposes not allowed to make its contribution to the design of buildings for public education owing to the system of official architects. As a result we have the provincial pseudo-architecture of the County Councils and the Municipalities, most of it a sight to put all heaven in a rage. In continental countries the best of living architects have been employed, and with their achievements in school design and decoration as well as functional fitness we cannot as yet begin to compare. The cultural loss in England is beyond statement. It is just dawning on us that if we wish the young to appreciate Art we should first have educational buildings which are works of art.

The main body of our community centre will be a large hall with a modern stage and cinema equipment, usually of not less than 2800 square feet, such as the Board of Education have sanctioned in Cambridgeshire; attached to the hall there will be a good kitchen. In our rural region this hall will, in size, amenity and conveniences, be easily the best hall for public purposes—for drama, music, the cinema, dances, meetings and festivals. The uses to be made of it by the senior school are clear—assembly, midday meal, music, dancing, drama, speech days, and the rest. But the hall must be more than a school hall in size—if it is twice the usual size all the better.

The remaining accommodation of our country community centre will fall into four groups:

(1) A site of at least 12 acres where the senior school has 240 pupils; better still 15 acres. There is a great need of spaciousness for our public buildings; and apart from the school garden, a rural community centre should have playing fields and a running track which will enable outdoor games throughout the year to form part of the recreational programme for the area.

(2) The classrooms for the use of the senior scholars in the day-time, about which I need say nothing except that it is time we realized that the square or oblong is not the only possible shape

for a classroom and that the circular classroom is at least as effective and is far more beautiful. In this connection I would stress the most imaginative use of colour in decoration.

(3) Rooms for practical activities. The minimum is a wood and metal workshop with the art room adjoining; a domestic science room, and (if a house is not available for the realistic acquirement of domestic crafts) a sitting room and a bedroom with a bath; a science laboratory and, if a separate engineering room is not to be had, an annex in which the internal combustion engine and electricity can be studied in their contemporary application to agriculture. Such a science laboratory should open straight out on to the school garden, or better still be placed in the centre of the school garden, with which it may then form an experimental observational and teaching unity. Finally, we should have a fully equipped gymnasium and at least an open-air swimming pool.

All these rooms for practical activities should be made large enough and equipped for adult use in the evenings as well as for use in the day-time by the senior school. This is an essential requirement.

(4) The adult block.

First comes the library, which will be the home of the county library and the school library—to be used by the senior school in the day-time and by young people and adults in the evening. It will be a silent room with provision for reading and study.

Secondly, an adult lecture room of about 800 square feet, with a common-room (of about 600 square feet) adjoining, both of them sacred to adult use. These will be the focal point of adult education in the evenings and even in the day-time. Here will meet university extension and other study groups; the debating society and union; committees of all kinds of local societies; the parish council of the central village. Round the walls cabinet lockers can be fixed and allotted to the main local societies for the storage of their documents and records. The common-room should have a hatch opening into it from the kitchen so that refreshments can be served, and there will be easy chairs and opportunity for silent games. The adult lecture room will be decorated and furnished so that it will look not like a classroom but a meeting place for young people and maturity—let us panel the walls with plywood, which is as cheap almost as plaster and much more beautiful and serviceable, and provide semi-easy chairs and a few tables; never educational tables or desks.

I have stated what I regard as the minimum. I think there is a need for a small committee room, and for a games room with a billiard table, table tennis and darts. A clubroom or hut for the very young people of fifteen to sixteen who have just left school is at least desirable, especially as a home for scouts and guides. Rural community centres should have a simple observatory, as accessible as for example the local inn, in which the country lad and girl and the older enthusiast can become universe-minded and acquire a valuable interest with as much naturalness as they learn to dance. Finally, I would add a place, of great architectural beauty, for silence and meditation. In it the senior school would assemble each day with the ritual of a corporate act accompanied by the hearing of the classic prose and poetry of the English Bible and by the great music of Europe. Our state educational institutions are classroom-ridden, lesson-ridden, text-book-ridden, given over to incessant didactic discourse and discursiveness. They lack ritual and rhythm and that kind of corporate ceremony in which the personality even of the young is freed and enhanced by the profoundly affecting dramatic combination of architecture, music, literature, and movement.

I cannot forbear to add that ideally the junior school of the central village or small town should form part of the community centre. Such a junior school, decorated and equipped with abandon and gaiety, should include a nursery classroom or rooms, a medical clinic and waiting rooms. Here would be the home of pre-natal and child welfare; of realistic child welfare instruction for the girls of the senior school; of the school medical service; of parental education and community education in health, especially by means of health clubs—in brief, a centre for the pursuit of health by education and preventive medicine.

Such a junior school would form a model on which the junior schools of the contributory villages would be formed; for I need not add that educationally the schools of all the villages forming the rural region should be regarded as an organic whole.

I shall be met with the query 'Can we afford all this?' We could, if we wished, and we ought to. Apart from the fact that our contemporary civilization is a prodigal misuse and waste of human and economic resources and ignoring the blindness that does not see that health and education are the chief instruments of racial preservation, there is the new fact that social services and social reconstruction on a vast scale are the only ways in which we can hope to use the practically limitless increment of wealth with which science and technology have potentially endowed us. We must rid ourselves of the infirmity of economy, and prepare ourselves boldly for an era, indefinitely long, of unremitting social reconstruction.

But much can even now be done within the four corners of the grant regulations of the Board of Education. The Board's new suggestions for school buildings disclose a remarkable advance, for in them the conception of the rural community centre or indeed the village college with the rural senior school as its basis is plainly set forth. Local education authorities are indeed invited to have this community ideal in their minds in designing rural senior schools. A commodious hall is rightly suggested as the first requisite; and then adequately large and equipped practical rooms, and a library. The suitability of the building and its amenities for evening use as a cultural and social centre are stressed. Though accommodation specially set aside for adult use is not mentioned, I do not doubt that the Board would be prepared to recognize for grant an adult lecture room and common-room as they have done in connexion with Village Colleges of Cambridgeshire.[1] To this extent, therefore, there is no financial obstacle to the realization of the senior school as the community centre for the area it serves.

Social progress is the substitution for one set of solved problems of a new and more significant set of problems making even greater

[1] There are now (1941) four, Sawston, Bottisham, Linton and Impington.

demands on human originality and energy. The solution of the economic problem waits no longer on knowledge but on an effort of political will and administration. Already the new order of leisure is with us and has become, with an imperativeness difficult to express, the major problem of human society.

Neither in Western Europe nor in America is there yet evidence of any community undertaking what is in our time, and will increasingly be, the task of the public authority—the provision of every facility that science and art can devise for the constructive use of leisure time. We need constantly to remind ourselves of the menace of aimless leisure amidst economic security, and of the decadence and disillusion that will arise with widespread intellectual and emotional unemployment. They would be even more tragic than the sufferings of the long era of restriction and over-worked poverty from which we are emerging. For the individual and for society it is the plain truth that, in the plenitude that lies before us, we must sublimate with infinite resource, or fail.

The grand task of education is frankly to convert society into a series of cultural communities. The most far-reaching development of education in this century will come from regarding it not only as a matter of psychology but also as the core of social and political philosophy so that education will be the fundamental principle and educational institutions the essential material of concrete social organization in city and countryside. Our communities, whether urban or rural, must be organized around their educational institutions. Education corporately administered is the principle of unity by which modern communities can be significantly integrated at any stage of culture in East or West. Unity or universalism on the basis of any metaphysical belief is no longer possible in the modern world; and such beliefs must increasingly remain the province of the individual and of autonomous associations within the community. Education as humanist philosophy and public policy, as the application at a maximum measure of science and art to the life of the individual and society, may well become as exciting as competition and war and, in the form ultimately of a planetary campaign, their social and racial equivalent.

The next great phase of social constructiveness may be near; if so, we may then hope that our towns may be reformed and indeed rebuilt. I venture to suggest that the proposals I have discussed in this brief paper may make it possible for us to preserve, for some time, side by side with urban civilization, a form of rural society, expressed in terms of the rural region, which will have a peculiar value in our own and indeed in every country in the world.

Comenius' visit to England, and the rise of Scientific Societies in the seventeenth century

By J. D. BERNAL, F.R.S.

Professor of Physics in the University of London

'It is inglorious to despair of progress.' This quotation from Johann Valentin Andreae[1] was chosen by Comenius to head his preface to the 'Great Didactic'. Comenius himself throughout his life never lost his faith in human progress and never ceased from contributing to it. The place of Comenius in the development of world culture is significant. He stands midway between the ordered but mystical world of the middle ages and the turbulent and practical world of modern Science and Industry. He carried in himself the highest ideals of both. It is only in these days that we can begin to appreciate the character of the man who did so much to herald the new age. For at least in its miseries and injustices the world of to-day is very like that of the Thirty Years' War, which dominated the central part of Comenius' life. He was, like so many of his distinguished compatriots to-day, a refugee, always sincerely attached to his native Moravia, always hoping to return there, and yet acquiring in his many travels a far wider loyalty to human beings in all countries and climates. What strikes the reader of Comenius almost more than anything else is the comprehensiveness of his outlook and the broadness of his sympathies.[2] This is even more surprising when we consider that his age was one of harsh and embittered controversies in every field of religion, learning, and politics; an age of religious persecution, of civil war, and of the conflict between the new awakening Science and the Philosophy of the Ancients. Comenius was not ignorant of these struggles but he refused to be bound by them. He took his own part but it was the part of humanity and not of sect.

The struggles of the seventeenth century, grim though they were, carried with them an atmosphere of hope and progress, which we

---

[1] Like Sir Thomas More, Andreae wrote a Utopia, "Christianopolis" (1619); it is described in L. Mumford's "Story of Utopias" (1923) and there is an English translation by F. E. Held (1916).   [2] See Note A.

see again to-day. As the battle moved from country to country, the centre of hope moved with it. Driven from the Czech lands and then from Poland, battered by the advance of the Counter-Reformation, the hopes of the pioneers of the new culture centred on Holland, England and Sweden. Comenius was to pass much of his latter days in these countries. In the first half of the seventeenth century, England was probably closer to continental thought than she has ever been since. The close commercial relations with Holland, the wanderings of political and religious refugees from the continent to England and back again, the common interests in rising trade and manufacture, led to a community of feeling and knowledge. The intellectual basis for the political and economic revolution that was to give England the leadership of the new world was laid by continental refugees to England such as Hartlib and Haak and by English refugees, traders and students abroad, such as Digby, Durie and Harvey. Already in the thirties of the century, England was seething with a ferment of political and cultural ideas which were to lead to the great revolution and the civil wars. The new rising and active populace of the great cities were more receptive to ideas and more anxious to put them into practice than they were to be for many years afterwards. The time of Comenius' visit was, therefore, opportune, but it had been too long delayed. In 1641 words and ideas were beginning to give way to arms and deeds. In English history, Comenius' visit lies obscured by the events which were immediately to follow it. Nevertheless we can now see how important it was, and though it did not achieve either then or afterwards its professed aims, it had a profound influence on the developments of Institutions, of Education and of Science.

Comenius came to England by invitation. That implies that what he had to give was already consciously desired by leading minds of the country, and indeed all of Comenius' principles fitted with the needs of the time. Where he excelled was in having in his own person the knowledge and experience that existed elsewhere scattered in many minds; and in having a burning faith in the practicability of what he propounded. In essence Comenius' mission was a religious one. He was perhaps the best exponent of the ideals of the Czech Brethren of the Unity, but where he excelled them was in his fervent desire to spread Christianity to a circle far wider than that of the elect, and in his practical conceptions of how this could be done. For him, Toleration, Peace and Justice were far more necessary parts of true religion and education than exhortation or force; true education was the means by which it should be spread. It was in studying education and practising it in the schools that Comenius came to make his greatest contribution, the discovery that education must proceed from an understanding of the needs and interest of pupils and that it must be based on the experience of life which children actually have. But that discovery led him further. In his epoch-making text-book 'Janua linguarum',[1] he attempted to give a balanced picture of the whole of human knowledge and practice. It was the first, and in point of comprehensiveness and simplicity, the best, of modern encyclopaedias, and it gave him the idea of the need to acquire knowledge from things and not from books.

In his great satirical work, 'The Labyrinth', he exposes, as Swift was to do after him, the follies and emptiness of existing learning, and yet he hoped that, by a reformation of that learning and by attention to practical human needs, these follies would be replaced by a true light. In this he was strongly influenced by Bacon, and though coming after Bacon, he really represented, far more than Bacon did, the link between mediaeval and modern knowledge. He had a much stronger feeling than Bacon or the men of the Renaissance, of community and of religion, and his sense of social justice enabled him to see the dangers of the pursuit of knowledge for individual enrichment. His own picture of knowledge, as given in his 'Physics', was still essentially mediaeval, but it contained in itself seeds of escape from the net of words by constant appeal to things. This appeal, he insisted throughout, needs to be made in an organized way. It was thus that he became the prophet and pioneer of the organization of scientific research. His own knowledge, expressed in his pansophic schemes, was of less importance to history than his insistence on the comprehensiveness and unity of all theory and practice.

[1] See Note B.

Comenius, like Harvey, is a transitional figure between mediaeval Aristotelianism and modern science. Though much of what he says is archaic, he attacks Aristotelian logic like any Glanvill again and again in books such as the 'Patterne of Universall Knowledge' (1651), the 'Natural Philosophy Reformed' (1651) and even in the 'Reformation of Schooles' (1642). His description of the 'pansophicall method' in the first of these has a strangely modern ring. It implies in Nature, he says, a 'perpetual Coherence, a perpetual Gradation, and a perpetual Uniformity'. There should be one system of knowledge, one method of study, and 'things are so conjoyn'd with things, as alwaies and everywhere the latter may seem of their own accord to arise out of the former'. This point of view embodied an appreciation of the coherence quality of established scientific truth, as well as an understanding of natural development and transitions which even the nineteenth century hardly achieved. Or again, the following passage from the 'Reformation of Schooles' illustrates how he criticized the application of formal logic to nature, his criticism being correct though his examples were quaint or even wrong.

For example, that Metaphysicall Theoreme, *Substantia non recepit magis et minus*, is neither true, nor if it be true is it of any use. For he that is fully growne up is more a man than an embryo is or an infant in the womb; an Eagle is more a bird than a Bat, and the Sunne is more light than the Moone.

And Comenius appreciated, too, the value of the quantitative approach to natural phenomena. In the 'Patterne' he says:

Truth is a solid thing; the more it is poysed and brandish'd the more purely it shines; nor is there any roome for Impostures, when all places are full of numbers, measures, ballances, and touchstones, nor aught admitted but what hath undergone severe and full examination.

Comenius' appreciation of the role of science in society comes out particularly clearly in his 'Via lucis', which, though partly written during his stay in London in 1641, did not appear till 1668 at Amsterdam. By that time the Royal Society had been fully constituted, and Comenius dedicated his book to 'the torchbearers of this enlightened age, members of the Royal Society of London, now bringing real philosophy to a happy birth'. While congratulating them on their efforts, he urged them not to neglect metaphysics and the general enlightenment of mankind.

Let us then assume [he said] that you, indefatigable investigators of Nature, have conquered her whole domain, so that with Solomon you understand the constitution of the world; the power of the elements; the beginning, the end, the intervening spaces of time; the changes of the solstices, the succession of the seasons; the circuit of the year and the positions of the stars; the natures of living things and the tempers of beasts; the powers of spirits and the thoughts of men; the various kinds of plants and the properties of roots; everything, in effect, that is either plain or obscure—let us assume all this, and then you must know that you have at last mastered but the alphabet of divine wisdom, but reached the threshold in the temple of God; and that his courts and secret places are only now upon your horizon.... We adjure you, then, who are priests in the realm of Nature, to press on your labours with all vigour; see to it that mankind is not for ever mocked by a philosophy empty, superficial, false, uselessly subtle.... We must say at once and plainly that the main political theories on which the present rulers of the world support themselves are treacherous quagmires, and the real causes of the generally tottering and indeed collapsing condition of the world. It is for you to show that errors are no more to be tolerated, even though they have the authority of long tradition...; you must show, not only to theologians, but also to politicians, that everything must be called back to Light and Truth.

Significantly enough, Comenius' optimism about the coming enlightenment of mankind was based on what we should to-day call an evolutionary outlook. The 'Via lucis' contains many fine passages describing the ascent of man from primitive savagery through the beginnings of the arts, to the classical period and so on to the writer's own time. This clear conception of social evolution was much to Comenius' credit, especially in view of the fact that the seventeenth century did not have and could not have had the backing and support which a knowledge of biological evolution gives it in our time. Lack of such knowledge was undoubtedly a limitation to Comenius' thought. It probably goes some way towards explaining his weakness for more or less bona fide chiliastic prophecies such as those of Kotter, Poniatowska and Drabić, which caused him so much unhappiness in his lifetime and about which some of his modern biographers, such as Keatinge, have made merry. Comenius was, in fact, not very sure about his time-scale. But if millenniarism was one of his doctrines, it only made him the more orthodox by the standards of the early Church, and millenniarism has a natural affinity with an ethic and a politic based on social and biological evolution. The 'Via lucis' is full of Isaiah-like prophetic writing about the coming illumination of humanity and its settlement in a state of world peace.

The last part of the 'Via lucis' is devoted to a detailed description of Comenius' practical proposals. 'For the Universal Light', he said, 'there are four requisites; Universal Books, Universal Schools, a Universal College, and a Universal Language.' H. G. Wells' 'Outline of History' is the kind of thing suggested by Comenius for his 'Panhistoria', and he would have recognized the partial achievement of his aim in all the inexpensive books of popular education of our day. His universal schools are not yet a reality throughout the world, but the conquest of illiteracy after the 1917 revolution in Russia would have appealed to his spacious mind. And in spite of his attachment to Latin, the Basic English and Esperanto movements would have been hailed by him as a great step in the right direction.

The object of Durie and Hartlib in inviting Comenius to England was primarily to use his already great influence to persuade Parliament to set up a Pansophic or Universal College in England and to make England the centre of the great restoration and improvement of knowledge and practice that they foresaw. Other sponsors had in view the more immediate practical question of reform and elementary schooling. To Comenius both of these were integral parts of his general scheme. The Pansophic College as a project was never anywhere realized; it combined in itself too many diverse elements. It was to be monastery, workshop and school in one. In the seventeenth century the learned man was, for all his good intentions, too far removed from practical life to lead the way to such a transformation of Arts and Technics. It is probable that even if the promoters of the Pansophic College had succeeded in creating such an institution, it would have remained a sterile anachronism. It is only now, with our far greater understanding of the relations of knowledge to practice, that any comprehensive organization of science can fruitfully be attempted. Nevertheless Comenius' visit did have fruitful results. It is not possible to trace any direct connexion between that visit and the foundation of the most vigorous and important of seventeenth-century scientific societies, the Invisible College or Royal Society; in any case it would be unprofitable to do so. The influence of Comenius was in the direction of its foundation. Many of its promoters had met Comenius on his visit to England and were acquainted with his writings. One of the greatest of the original founders, Robert Boyle, was a man with a temperament and motives not unlike those of Comenius himself. The revelation of the knowledge and wisdom of God and the Propagation of the Gospel to the Heathen were alike the leading motives of the great educator and the great scientist.

To us, still confused by the nineteenth-century conflicts between Religion and Science, it is difficult to see the extremely close relation which existed in the seventeenth century between mystical, 'experimental' Christianity, hard practical self-help, and experimental science. Yet a study of the personalities of the seventeenth-century scientists shows all these elements present and indeed the combination is the keynote of Puritanism—in the conversions of men like Boyle, Pascal and Steno, and in the poetry of Milton and Marvell. The two roots of modern science, the study of Nature and of human trades, both appeared as eminently religious objects to the Puritan, the first because it would reveal the glory and wisdom of Divine Providence, the second because it could only lead to an increase of sobriety and godly industry. But the religion of the early scientists was not to be united in an organized way, as Comenius would have wished it, with their science. It was, in fact, by a wise necessity that in the scientific societies of the seventeenth century, religion and metaphysical philosophy were alike excluded. The later phases of the Commonwealth in England disabused men of any hope in the rule of the saints.

Restoration England was too cynical and worldly to accept the full implication of Comenius' ideas, but it did accept enough of them to make possible the material side of the progress which he so earnestly desired. But in the twentieth century we have lived to see how vain that material progress is without peace and social justice, and how science must be organized for human welfare and not for destruction. The message of Comenius was important in the building up of modern science, but it still needs to be heard to prevent that science from destroying more than it has built.

Note A. Comenius' awareness of the social injustices of his time is well shown in the following bitter passages from the *Labyrinth*. They occur when human wrongs are being righted at the court of the Queen of Worldly Wisdom:

Page 255. Sec. 9. The Humble Supplications of the Poor.

"Now the poor of all ranks came forth with a supplication, in which they complained of the great inequality in the world, and that others had abundance while they suffered want. They begged that this might in some fashion be righted. After the matter had been weighed, it was decreed that the poor should be told in answer that H.R.M. wished indeed that all should have as much comfort as they could themselves desire, but that the glory of the kingdom demanded that the light of some should shine above that of others. Therefore, in accordance with the order established in the world, it could not be otherwise than that as Fortuna had her castle, so also should Industria have her workshops full of people. But this was granted them, that each one who was not idle might raise himself from poverty by whatever means he could or knew."

Page 258. Sec. 13. Supplications of the Subjects (i.e. serfs).

"Not long afterwards envoys of the subjects, tradesmen, and peasants came forward, and complained that those who were over them wished nothing but to drink their sweat; for they ordered them to be so driven and harassed that bloody sweat ran down them. And those whom the lords employed for such purposes were all the more cruel to them, that they also might obtain a small dish at their expense. And as a proof of this they incontinently showed countless weals, stripes, scars, and wounds; and they asked for mercy. And it appeared evident that this was an injustice, and therefore should be stopped; but as the rulers had been permitted to govern by means of these servants, it appeared that they were the guilty ones; they were therefore summoned to appear. Summonses were therefore sent out to all the royal, princely, and lordly councillors, regents, officials, stewards, collectors, writers, judges, and so forth, informing them that they must appear without fail. They obeyed the order, but against one accusation they brought forward ten. They complained of the laziness of the peasants, their disobedience, insubordination, conceit, their mischievous ways as soon as their bit was even slightly loosened, and other things. After these men had been heard, the whole matter was again considered by the council. Then the subjects were told that, as they either did not love and value the favour of their superiors, or were unable to obtain it, they must become used to their ferocity; for thus must it be in the world, that some rule and others serve. Yet it was granted them, that if by willingness, compliance, and true attachment to their superiors and rulers they could gain their favour, they should be allowed to enjoy it."

Note B. It is interesting to observe the distribution of interest which Comenius uses in the 'Janua'; thus of the 98 Sections of the body of the work, 30 are devoted to Natural History, 16 to Arts and Trades, 20 to Learning and Culture, 5 to Social Life, 10 to Ethics, 11 to Politics, and 6 to Religion. It would be interesting to see what the distribution would be in any contemporary attempt to give a comprehensive view of modern knowledge.

Comenius and the Invisible College (1645—1662)

By R. FITZGIBBON YOUNG

The Hon. Robert Boyle, in a letter to Tallents dated 20 February 1646, writes: 'The corner stones of the invisible or (as they term themselves) the philosophical college do now and then honour me with their company.'

In a letter to Samuel Hartlib, dated 8 March 1647, Boyle says: 'You interest yourself so much in the Invisible College.'

Birch in his 'Life of Boyle' (1744) writes: 'The Invisible College probably refers to that assembly of learned and curious gentlemen who at length gave birth to the Royal Society.'[1]

The significance of the word 'invisible', as applied to the informal meetings of scientists which were held in London and Oxford from 1645 to 1660, appears on a first view to be quite simple. It seems appropriately to describe a college or association on a voluntary basis without a charter of incorporation, or a fixed meeting-place, as contrasted with a body such as the Royal College of Physicians (1516), which had a Royal Charter and permanent headquarters in London. However, even a cursory examination of the contemporary use of the term 'invisible' shows that it had subtle and rather elusive associations and that it is by no means easy to delimit its precise meaning as applied by Boyle and his friends to the 'Philosophical College'.

As I endeavour to show below,

(a) It may be an Italian 'concetto' adopted by Boyle from the name of a literary Academy at Cremona.

(b) It may have been borrowed from the contemporary critics and opponents of the 'invisible' Rosicrucians, such as J. V. Andreae (1586–1654).[2]

(c) It may be a reminiscence of an elaborate play on the word 'invisible' in a comedy entitled 'The Bird in a Cage' (1633) by James Shirley (1596–1666).

(d) It may be a name devised by Theodore Haak (1605–1690), an exile from the Palatinate who met Comenius on 21 September 1641, on his arrival in England, and who started the 'Invisible College' in London in 1645, containing an allusion (on the

---

[1] Boyle's 'Works' (ed. T. Birch), I. xi and xvii; T. Birch, 'History of the Royal Society', I. 2.   [2] 'Allg. Deutsche Biographie,' I, 441.

analogy of the 'Invisible Church' of the Puritans) to Comenius' plan of 1641–42 for a great International College in England for scientific research to be called 'Collegium Lucis'.

(e) Boyle and Haak who corresponded with Father Marin Mersenne, may have been thinking of the informal 'college of science' kept by Mersenne in his cell at the Minorite friary in Paris.

I shall now discuss these points in order:

In the sixteenth and seventeenth centuries there were in Italy literary, and in some instances also scientific, academies in most towns of any size. Many of these societies had far-fetched and fanciful names. It is accordingly not surprising to find, in view of the wide vogue of metaphors drawn from vision and light in the seventeenth century, that there was an 'Accademia degli Invisibili' at Cremona. The date of its foundation is unknown, but it was in existence in 1622.[1]

There was also at Syracuse an 'Accademia della Setta dei Filosofi' in 1640.[2]

It is known that the Honourable Robert Boyle (1627–91) spent the winter of 1641–42 in Florence and he also spent some time in Rome in 1642.[3] It is therefore quite possible that he may have taken the names 'Invisible' and 'Philosophical' from these Italian Academies.

The Rosicrucian organizations which sprang up in South-Western Germany early in the seventeenth century were to a great extent secret societies, laying special emphasis on certain mysterious scientific truths which they claimed to possess.[4]

The famous Lutheran divine and thinker, Johann Valentin Andreae (1586–1654) of Stuttgart, at first sympathized with the Rosicrucians, but later reverted to Lutheran orthodoxy and ridiculed their pretensions in a book entitled 'Turris Babel sive iudiciorum de fraternitate roseae crucis chaos', published in 1619. In it he repeatedly refers to the Rosicrucians as 'The Invisibles',

---

[1] Cinelli, 'Biblioteca Volante' (Cremona, 1622), IV. 515; L'Arisi, 'Cremona literata' (1741), III. 301.

[2] Maylender, 'Storia delle accademie d' Italia' (Bologna, 1929), v. 167.

[3] 'D.N.B.' VI. 119.

[4] 'Fama fraternitatis' (Kassel, 1614); 'Confessio fraternitatis' (1615); E. Peuckert, 'Die Rosenkreutzer' (Jena, 1928), pp. 33–40, 59–228.

in reference to their supposed claim to be able to render themselves invisible, and to their secret meetings.[1]

Theodore Haak (1605–90), a native of the Rhenish Palatinate
who had settled in England about 1625, kept closely in touch with
intellectual developments on the continent, especially in South-
Western Germany. He must have known about Andreae's attacks
on the Rosicrucians. As it was Haak who initiated the informal
meetings of the 'Philosophical College' in London in 1645,[2] it is
quite possible that it was also he who coined the name 'invisible'.
If this be the case, it affords a classic instance of a word, originally
applied in derision, being converted into a term of honour.

In Act IV, Scene I of 'The Bird in a Cage'[3] (1633), by James
Shirley (1596–1666), the following ballad is sung by Morello:

> There was an invisible foxe by chance
> Did meet two invisible geese[4]
> He led 'em a fine invisible dance
> For a hundred crowns a peece.
> Invisible all but his head he would goe,
> But when it came to be tryed,
> Not only his head which was left, he did show
> But a faire paire of heels beside.
> Invisible since their wits have been,
> But yet there is hope of either;
> Their wits and their crowns may return againe
> Invisible altogether.[5]

Shirley was a Roman Catholic and a protégé of Queen Henrietta
Maria, so it is possible that in his play on the word 'invisible'

---

[1] In the dedication of his 'Turris Babel' (1619) to Hein of Rostock, Andreae writes:
'Vide, optime Heinie, quibus rationibus contra fraternitatem illam invisibilem utar';
cf. also Peuckert, *op. cit.* pp. 206, 212, 415–599. Leibniz refers contemptuously to the
Rosicrucians' claim to be able to render themselves invisible: 'Fratres Roseae Crucis
ficticios fuisse suspicor. ... Nam scire, quae remotis locis fiunt, invisibilem sese atque
invulnerabilem reddere, haud dubie nugaria vel potius irrisoria sunt.' Arnauld and
Nicole, in their famous Port-Royal 'Logic' (1662), make some very uncomplimentary
observations about the Rosicrucian 'enthusiasts'.

[2] 'D.N.B.' XXIII. 412; Weld, 'A History of the Royal Society', 1; T. Birch, 'History
of the Royal Society', I. 2.

[3] 'A Comedie as it hath been produced at the Phoenix in Drury Lane' (London, 1633).

[4] The game of Fox and Geese is mentioned in Shackerley Marmion's (1603–39)
comedy, 'The Fair Companion' (1633), II. v. 'Let him sit in the shop...and play
at fox and geese with the foreman.'

[5] Possibly an allusion to William Prynne (1600–69), the author of 'Histriomastix
or the Players' scourge and Actors' tragedy' (1631), who at this time (1633) was a
prisoner in the Tower awaiting trial by the Court of Star Chamber, or to some contemporary 'confidence' tricksters.

he was poking fun at the 'invisible' Rosicrucians, or at the Puritans and their 'Invisible Church', or perhaps at both.

It is certain that many English literary men of this period knew about the Rosicrucians and the criticisms on them by Andreae and others through George Weckherlin (1584–1653), a German poet and man of letters from Stuttgart, who after acting as 'Cammer-Secretary' to the Duke of Wurtemberg from 1614 to 1623, migrated to England, where he served as Under-Secretary of State from 1624 to 1641.

In 1644 he was made Secretary for Foreign Affairs to the Joint Committee of the Two Kingdoms, and he held this office till 1649, when he was succeeded by John Milton.[1] Weckherlin must have known about Andreae and his criticisms of the Rosicrucians, as Andreae was Court Chaplain to Weckherlin's former patron, the Duke of Wurtemberg.

Jan Amos Comenius (1592–1670), the famous Bohemian philosopher and educationist, who was invited to London in September 1641 by a group of members of both Houses of Parliament to advise regarding the establishment of a college for scientific research, composed a treatise on his scheme in the winter of 1641–42, entitled 'Via lucis', which was circulated in manuscript among his English friends.[2] In some of his later works he refers to his projected scientific College as 'Collegium Lucis'.[3] It is quite possible that Theodore Haak, who had been one of the principal supporters of the Comenian plan for a scientific Academy in London in 1641–42, may have regarded the informal meetings of scientists which he organized in 1645, as the nucleus of a future State college for scientific research, and may half humorously have described it to Boyle and others as the 'Invisible College of Light' on the analogy of the 'Invisible Church' of the Puritans.[4]

---

[1] 'D.N.B.' LX. 128; 'Allg. Deutsche Biographie', XLI. 375.
[2] R. Fitzgibbon Young, 'Comenius in England' (1932), pp. 6, 16, 19; 'Via lucis' (1668), Chapter XVIII.
[3] J. Kvačala, 'Die pädagogische Reform des Comenius in Deutschland', II. 286. 'Optatum nobis pridem collegium lucis' (excerpted from Comenius' 'Sermo Secretus' written at Saros Patak in Hungary in 1651).
[4] E.g. 'Scottish Confession of Faith' (1561), XVI: 'This (the Catholik) kirk is invisible.' Cf. W. Chillingworth, 'The Religion of Protestants' (1638), Answers IV. §53 and V.§56. In a letter of 1 March 1663 to Baron von Boineburg of Mainz, Theodore

It is possible that Boyle and Haak were also thinking of the 'Invisible College' kept by Father Marin Mersenne (1588–1648) in his cell at the Minorite friary in the Place Royale in Paris, where he was constantly visited by eminent scientists with whom he also corresponded.[1] Thomas Hobbes (1588–1679), describing in his old age in 1672 the impression made on him by Mersenne in 1640, writes:

> 'Adfuit e Minimis Mersennus, fidus amicus,
> Vir doctus, sapiens eximieque bonus
> Cuius cella scholis erat omnibus anteferenda.
> Circa Mersennum convertebatur ut axem
> Unumquodque aetis sidus in orbe suo.'
>
> (T. Hobbes, *Opera Philosophica*, I. 149.)

Francis Bacon, in a famous passage of his 'Novum Organum' (1620), criticizes those philosophers who constrain words, not things: 'verba constringunt, non res'. It is evident, however, that it is no easy matter to define the connotation which the word 'invisible' had for a cultured Englishman in 1645, and that, in attempting to do so, we are concerned not merely with words, but with intricate and subtle associations of thought.

Haak, writing from London, describes the foundation of the Royal Society in 1662. He refers to the earlier 'Invisible College' as 'cette compagnie'. 'Commercii epistol. Leibnitiani tomus prodromus' (Göttingen, 1745), II. 1085.

[1] 'Correspondance du Père Marin Mersenne,' publiée par Madame Paul Tannery, I & II (1617–1630), Paris, 1932 & 1937.

Comenius and Harvard

By J. B. CONANT
President of Harvard University

The learned world and particularly the profession of teaching are grateful to the University of Cambridge for observing the Comenius Tercentenary. Harvard University has a peculiar indebtedness to Jan Comenius. According to a persistent tradition, he was offered the headship of Harvard College within five years of its founding; probably he was approached on that subject by John Winthrop, Junior, Governor of Connecticut and Overseer of Harvard College, who like Comenius was a friend of Samuel Hartlib. In any case, the great Moravian was looked up to by the founders of Harvard as the principal authority on education in Europe. His improved textbooks were used both in Harvard College and in the early Grammar Schools of New England. In our Library there is a copy of the famous 'Janua linguarum' with the autograph of one of our Indian students on the fly-leaf.[1]

Now, after the lapse of three hundred years, we wish to associate Harvard University with the just tribute that you are making to the life and work of Comenius. He conferred a double benefit upon education, first by his impatience with mere traditionalism and pedantry, and secondly by his own important and original contributions to the principles of education. The spirit of Comenius should make possible in every generation that fresh envisaging of educational problems which he, against overwhelming odds, forced upon his contemporaries.

As the founders of our 'University in the Wilderness' in their poverty and struggle looked across the sea for inspiration to this great scholar and teacher of the Czech nation, so, in the midst of a no less difficult struggle, we wish through you, to express our gratitude for all that Comenius and other great scholars of that brave and intelligent nation have contributed to learning and to civilization.

[1] See on, p. 55.

Comenius' Life and Work in its Historical Setting

By O. ODLOŽILÍK

formerly Professor of Czech History in the Caroline University at Prague,
now Lecturer at Columbia University, New York

Comenius chassé de Moravie par les féroces Espagnols, y perdit la patrie, et y gagna...
le monde. J'entends un sens unique d'universalité. D'un cœur et d'un esprit immense
il embrassa et toute science et toute nation. Par tous pays, Pologne, Hongrie, Suède,
Angleterre, Hollande, il alla enseignant: premièrement la paix, deuxièmement le
moyen de la paix, l'universalité fraternelle.

> Jules Michelet, 'Nos Fils' (Paris, 1869).

The place of Comenius in the history of education, therefore, is one of commanding
importance. He introduces and dominates the whole modern movement in the field
of elementary and secondary education. His relation to our present teaching is
similar to that held by Copernicus and Newton toward modern science, and Bacon
and Descartes toward modern philosophy.

> N. Murray Butler, 'The Place of Comenius in the History of Education'
> (Syracuse, N.Y. 1892).

In my subsequent journey round the world [in 1914–18] the 'Bequest' of Comenius,
together with the Kralice Bible of the Bohemian Brethren was for me a daily memento,
national and political.

> T. G. Masaryk, 'The Making of a State' (Prag, 1925).

I. INTRODUCTION

John Amos Komenský (Comenius) was born on 28 March 1592
in Moravia and died on 15 November 1670 in Amsterdam.

During his lifetime Europe passed through a series of grave conflicts and devastating wars. Conditions changed profoundly, not
only in the Kingdom of Bohemia, but over all the continent of
Europe. A man who had been born in the last decade of the
sixteenth century, in an atmosphere of comparative tranquillity,
and upon whose manhood the long and merciless war cast its
shadow, was not easily understood by the young generation and
passed away almost unnoticed. For some time uncertainty pre-
vailed concerning the year of Comenius' death, and the year 1671
was accepted by some biographers instead of the correct date.

Of his almost fourscore years more than half was spent in exile.
Comenius shared the lot of thousands of refugees whom Emperor
Ferdinand II drove from Bohemia and Moravia after his victory

41

over the Bohemian insurrection on the White Mountain in 1620. Despite unfavourable conditions Comenius worked assiduously in various fields and attained great fame in his own day. 'He did not toil in vain'—said R. H. Quick in his brilliant sketch of Comenius' life—'and historians of education have agreed in ranking him among the most influential as well as the most noble-minded of the Reformers.'

There is no doubt that as a champion of new methods in education Comenius became widely known among his contemporaries. In modern times historians of education have revived interest in his life and work. The rapid progress of studies and the growth of literature concerning Comenius and his ideas went hand in hand with the improvement of education in the modern age. The time has come for a close examination of the other subjects of his studies and deliberations. His life was eventful and his biography is full of unforeseen turns and dramatic episodes. The present upheavals, accompanied by the endless migration of peoples whom a conqueror has deprived of their homes, have sharpened our insight and disposed us to make a new scrutiny of both the hopes and sorrows of the exiled scholar and thinker.

II. KOMENSKÝ THE CZECH

Nor can I forget thee, thou Czech and Moravian nation, my native land....
  Comenius, 'The Bequest of the Unity of Brethren' (1650).

Comenius was the most prominent representative of the Czech people in the seventeenth century. Both the plight and the noble aspirations of his countrymen were reflected in his life and work. Among his contemporaries he held a position like that of John Hus in the fifteenth century and T. G. Masaryk in the modern era. His ideas and writings rank among the finest products of the Czech mind.

Like Hus and Masaryk Comenius was of humble parentage and owed his rise to prominence solely to education. The original home of his family was the small village of Komna in South-Eastern Moravia—hence the name Komenský which has become famous in its latinized form Comenius. He himself was most likely born in Nivnice and spent part of his childhood in Uherský Brod and in several other places. In the entourage of a Moravian nobleman, Kunovský of Kunovice, he visited Germany. In 1611 he matriculated at the University of Herborn in Nassau. After two years he left for Heidelberg and completed there the course of his education. After his return to Moravia he was active as schoolmaster in the town of Přerov and later as a minister of the Church. In normal times and conditions his career would have culminated in his ordination and in his appointment to the pastorate of a flourishing congregation at Fulnek, on the border of Moravia and Silesia.

Soon after his ordination, however, an insurrection flared up in the Kingdom of Bohemia. Though its immediate causes were of local importance it soon assumed the character of a prelude to a European conflagration. Like Czechoslovakia in the thirties of the present century so Bohemia in the early seventeenth century was a testing ground of conflicting forces. The issues of the conflict in Comenius' time were both religious and constitutional. In 1526 the country of John Hus did not effectively oppose the accession of Ferdinand I of the House of Hapsburg to the throne. Thus the seed of discord had been sown on Bohemian soil. The dynasty remained faithful to the Latin Church and promoted the Roman Catholic religion in all its domains in Central Europe, in Austria, Bohemia and Hungary. But the Bohemian nobility as well as the people followed in the footsteps of John Hus; they embraced the Protestant creed and maintained lively connexions with their co-religionists in other parts of Europe.

This difference in religion thwarted all collaboration between the ruler and the leading class of the Czech people. Moreover, the nobility viewed with jealous eye the attempts of the dynasty to strengthen its position in the country and to curtail the prerogatives of the Estates. Religious freedom was considered the foremost privilege of the free citizens of the kingdom. With the turn of the tide in the struggle between the Catholics and Protestants all over Europe the desire grew in Bohemia about the year 1600 for a solemn confirmation of liberty in matters of religion and for a written guarantee of peace in the country. In 1609 the effort of the Protestant nobility had been crowned with success. The ailing

Emperor Rudolph II issued a charter, known as 'the letter of Majesty', by which religious freedom was granted to the inhabitants of Bohemia.

There was, however, much unrest in Europe in the early seventeenth century and Bohemia was not spared. Peace in the country was of short duration. In less than a decade—events moved more slowly in those days than in our century—disputes over 'the letter of Majesty' and over supplementary agreements of the Protestant and Catholic nobility had created such an embitterment that a clash became inevitable. The trial and the 'defenestration'[1] of leaders of the Catholic group by spokesmen of the Protestant nobility in May 1618 inaugurated a rebellion in Bohemia. After two years of struggle the Emperor, acting as defender of his dynastic interests as much as of the positions of the Church, secured victory over the revolting nobility and established himself firmly in the country. For a great majority of the inhabitants of Bohemia and Moravia the day of the victory of Imperial troops on the White Mountain (8 November 1620) became the turning-point in their life. Quite appropriately a contemporary Czech chronicler called the White Mountain 'the origin and the door of all miseries and calamities that have befallen the Czech nation'.

The Unity of Bohemian Brethren, to which Comenius belonged, incurred the wrath of the Emperor earlier than other Protestant communions both for its close connexion with the Calvinists in various European countries and for the participation of its prominent members in the uprising. Not only against persons of rank but also against its clergy were several Imperial decrees directed, portending storm and persecution. In 1621 Comenius lost his home—Fulnek was set on fire by the Spanish mercenaries, destroying not only his house but also his library and manuscripts of several of his works. For several years he lived in constant fear and anxiety, changing frequently his place of abode.

The Bohemian insurrection put in motion an avalanche of enmities and local conflicts. It passed into a European conflagra-

---

[1] The term 'defenestration' refers to the fact that on 23 May 1618, the Chief Councillors of the Emperor actually were thrown out of the windows of the Castle of Prague, which was the signal for the revolt of the Czech nobility against the Hapsburg dynasty.

tion 'unique in its length, its constant shifting of scene and motive, its dreariness and ferocity'. For thirty years Imperial troops remained on the battlefields, opposed successively either by armies of individual rulers or by coalitions of the foes of the House of Hapsburg. With each Imperial victory the pressure on Bohemia and Moravia and its population increased. After the promulgation of a series of decrees, known as The Renewed Land Ordinance, in 1627, even the mountainous districts of North-Eastern Bohemia offered no safe refuge. So early in 1628 Comenius left Bohemia with hundreds of members of the Unity and settled in Leszno in Poland. Thus—to use the words of Jules Michelet—he lost his country and he found the world.

The town of Leszno became the centre of the exiled members of the Unity from Bohemia and Moravia. They lived there under the protection of the Polish noble family of Leśczyński, never losing hope in the ultimate defeat of the House of Hapsburg and the restoration of Bohemian liberties. Leszno became the new home of Comenius. He lived there among his countrymen and returned there after journeys abroad or prolonged residences in various countries, in England, Sweden or Hungary. The destruction of Leszno during the Swedish-Polish war in 1656, surpassing in its effect and dimensions the sack of Fulnek by the Spaniards, terminated abruptly the sojourn of Comenius in Poland. He accepted an invitation from Amsterdam and lived there 'on the shore of the Great Sea' until he died.

As a bishop of the Unity he was connected with its dispersed members by the bond of mutual love and co-ordinated his work to the interests of his Church and his nation. It would be difficult to understand Comenius' schemes and activities without a knowledge of his relation to the groups of exiles from Bohemia and Moravia and of his participation in the struggle for the restoration of Bohemian independence. He never severed the ties binding him to his native land, and directed his efforts to its liberation. The story of his life thus differs from the simple and uneventful biographies of most of his learned contemporaries, whom the storm of wrath and the prolonged hostilities never drove from their homes. Though he was several times offered positions, promising both substantial financial aid and a haven of rest, he never yielded to a longing for ease and for the end of his wanderings which would have been very understandable. Like a prophet and herald of hope, alternating with dejection and disappointment, he accompanied his people on the tortuous path leading through the labyrinth of war and social confusion. Up to the end of his days he remained a loyal citizen of the Kingdom of Bohemia, whose gate, as he often complained at the end of his life, had been closed for ever to him by the implacable tyrant.

For more than two decades prominent noblemen from Bohemia and Moravia stood in the forefront and directed the course of the struggle for the restoration of their country's independence. They participated in diplomatic activities, often helping to bring together the enemies of the House of Hapsburg and to prepare combined attacks on its domains and strategic positions. They offered their services to countries which waged war against the Emperor. They mustered regiments of volunteers from the ranks of their exiled countrymen and commanded them in battle. They fought under Dutch, Danish and Swedish banners, linking their cause with the anti-Hapsburg front. On several occasions they entered Bohemia and Moravia with foreign troops and encouraged their countrymen by their proclamations and deeds to resist more effectively the merciless conqueror of their country, whose real aim was the domination of Europe. The percentage of Czech officers and soldiers was high especially in the Swedish armies, which operated for almost twenty years in Germany and Central Europe, harassing the Imperial troops and preventing the Emperor from consolidating his gains. They kept alive the spirit of opposition to the 'new order' which the Hapsburgs introduced in the conquered kingdoms by force, executions, confiscations of property and banishment of opponents.

Comenius was not silent during this struggle for life or death. He did not wield the sword, but his pen was a mighty weapon in the defence of the common cause. In several writings in Czech he voiced the grief and anxiety of his people after the catastrophic end of the rebellion or in the periods of growing preponderance of Imperial armies over the Protestant forces. With prophetical words, taken as a rule from the books of the Old Testament, he welcomed powerful opponents of the House of Hapsburg and of its lust for world domination. In the hour of decision he became the only spokesman of the free Czechs, and he entreated the Swedish delegates at the peace conference to secure from the Imperial envoys tolerable terms for the exiled Czechs and for those in the occupied country who had resisted the pressure upon mind and conscience and remained faithful to their creed. He laboured in vain. Ignoring their solemn pledges, the Swedes accepted at the decisive moment a compromise and left Bohemia to the mercy of the Hapsburg ruler. They thus strengthened enormously the position of that dynasty which had provoked the long struggle by its intolerant attitude towards people of other creeds, and had mainly been responsible for the horrors of the war.

In the anguish of his soul Comenius announced to his dispersed countrymen the failure of his efforts and raised his voice to pronounce a high prophecy of the return of a more propitious age. The often quoted words from 'The Bequest of the Unity of Brethren': 'I trust God that after the passing of the storm of wrath which our sins brought down upon our heads, the rule of thine affairs shall again be restored to thee, O Czech people'—comforted the decimated ranks of the exiles. With them in mind Comenius worked for more than twenty years. He presented the world with a complete edition of his educational works, and in various books saved from extinction the ideas and the spirit which had permeated Czech spiritual life in the period of independence.

After more than two hundred and fifty years the prophecy of Comenius inspired T. G. Masaryk, on Dutch soil, to the struggle for liberation of Czechoslovak people. He inscribed Comenius' words on his revolutionary banner as well as at the head of his first message to the independent people, read in December 1918. Thus the indefatigable zeal and effort of Comenius was revived and linked up with the resurrection of the Czechs and their reunion with the Slovak people.

III. Komenský the Baconian

Here give me leave...to recommend to your favour the noble endeavours of two great and publique spirits who have laboured much for truth and peace, I meane Comenius and Duraeus; both famous for their learning, piety and integrity, and not unknown, I am sure, by the fame of their works to many of this honourable, pious and learned assembly.

John Gauden, 'The Love of Truth and Peace' (a sermon preached before the House of Commons, 29 November 1640).

During the years of uncertainty, after the promulgation of the Imperial decrees against Protestant ministers, Comenius was not able to attend publicly and regularly to his pastoral duties. He lived on the secluded estates of wealthy patrons of the persecuted clergy and devoted his time to study and literary activity. 'The Labyrinth of the World and the Paradise of the Heart', accessible to modern readers in a fine translation by Count Francis Lützow, is the best of the books and treatises which Comenius wrote in those critical years. During the last few months of his stay in the mountains of North-Eastern Bohemia he began to work on a book on education. He completed it in Leszno. The 'Great Didactic' was written in Czech because it was intended primarily for Czech educators, upon whose shoulders the new organization of schools was to rest after the liberation of Bohemia and Moravia. Only in 1657 did Comenius publish a Latin version of the book in the magnificent folio of 'The Complete Didactic Works'.

The 'Great Didactic' linked Comenius' work in his native land with his activities in exile. It indicated that in the early thirties of the seventeenth century the desire to reform education overshadowed all other interests in Comenius' mind. Simultaneously with the theoretical treatises on education there grew under his hands a school-book which met with an enormous and immediate success. It appeared in Leszno with the title 'Janua linguarum reserata'. In an autobiographical work ('Continuatio fraternae admonitionis') Comenius described the reception of the 'Janua' in the following words: 'From the learned in various lands there came to me letters giving me joy at my new discovery and in divers ways encouraging me to yet bolder enterprise.' The 'Janua' was intended as an introduction to the study of Latin. It was based on the principle that the understanding and the tongue should advance in parallel lines and that in the study of languages mechanical memorizing of words should be replaced by the teaching of words through things. It inaugurated a new era in the teaching of Latin and made a triumphal procession through Europe. It was known in twelve European languages and in Asia it appeared in Arabic, Turkish, Persian and even Mongolian.

On the title page of the first edition of the 'Janua' we can see a sentence which Comenius found in the preface to Bacon's 'Novum Organum' and used as a motto. Thus he acknowledged his indebtedness to the English thinker and presented his work as a continuation of the latter's effort to advance learning. If we look for parallels to the relation between Comenius and Bacon we must either go back to the middle ages and study Wyclif's influence on John Hus, or proceed to the modern age and consider Masaryk's predilection for English and American philosophy. In all these cases an affinity between English and Czech thought, and the desire of the leading Czech thinkers to compensate for German influences, acted as a stimulus.

As the author of the 'Janua' Comenius quickly became known in the British Isles. Its first edition, 'The Gate of Tongues Unlocked and Opened', was prepared for press by a French refugee John Anchoran and was published under his name in 1631 'in behalfe of the most illustrious Prince Charles and of the British, French and Irish youth'. The name of Comenius was only affixed to the preface, so that some confusion existed as to the authorship of the work.

Soon after the publication of the 'Janua' it became known to what 'bolder enterprise' Comenius had been encouraged by the admirers of his new method. He contemplated a book in which not only *words*, as was the case in the 'Janua', but also *facts*, would be classified and arranged according to their affinity. Thus the reader was to be presented with a survey of all human knowledge, which was to serve as 'a kind of Antidote-Universal to ignorance, misunderstanding, hallucinations and errors'. It was the author's desire to produce a work for which there was no parallel either in the past or in contemporary literature. During the years of exile he had become well acquainted with the causes of unrest in war-torn Europe, and he sought for remedies and guarantees of stability. A reconciliation of churches and a reform of education were in his opinion the prerequisites of durable peace. He therefore planned his new work not as a mere survey of data and facts, but wished to incorporate in it all that was 'necessary for the furtherance of felicity in this and the future life, whether of knowledge or faith, action or aspiration'.

The combination of purely theoretical interests with the aims of reform corresponded to the exiled scholar's state of mind. His work was an integral part of the heroic effort of the émigrés from Bohemia and Moravia to regain the independence of their kingdom. He wished to join hands, not with dispassionate writers, but with the architects of the new world to be erected on the ruins of the old. Though fascinating in itself, this combination proved to be an unsurmountable obstacle and the main cause of his failure. For several years, however, both Comenius and his friends cherished hopes of success of what they called 'Pansophy'. Words of encouragement were coming especially from London. Samuel Hartlib, whose name also appeared at the end of the preface to Anchoran's edition of the 'Janua', took genuine interest in the pansophic scheme. Being himself of foreign extraction and naturalized, he assumed the role of a mediator between English and continental scholars. Several members of Hartlib's circle shared with Comenius banishment from their home countries and the hard lot of exile. Hartlib was responsible both for the publication of a 'specimen of pansophy' ('Conatuum Comenianorum Praeludia') in Oxford in 1637, and for the invitation of Comenius to London in 1641.

Comenius arrived in England in September 1641 and left for Holland at the end of June 1642. During his stay in London he lived in the eastern part of the City and frequented ordinarily the congregation in the Dutch Church (Austin Friars). Soon after his arrival he was introduced to prominent English divines and scholars. James Ussher, Archbishop of Armagh; John Williams, Bishop of Lincoln and later Archbishop of York; Robert Greville, second Lord Brooke; John Pym, the prominent member of the Long Parliament; and many others, were interested in his ideas.

He met also Hartlib's intimate friend the Scottish divine John Durie (Duraeus), who for several years worked for the reconciliation of all Protestant churches. There was a perfect harmony between the three men. John Durie spoke of it in a letter to their patron Sir Cheney Colepeper in the following way: 'Though our taskes be different yet we are all three in a knowledge of one another's labours and can hardly be without one another's helpe and assistance.'

What Comenius and his patrons contemplated has been recorded in the eighteenth chapter of the book 'Via lucis' ('The Way of Light'), written in London in the winter of 1641–42. He planned an international academy with resident and corresponding members. As the headquarters he recommended a place 'to which, by the aid of navigation, access shall be easy from every country of the world, and from which in turn communication can be made to every country'. He recommended England for the following reasons:

We may say this first because we remember the heroic adventure of the Englishman Drake, who by voyaging five times round the whole world, gave us a prelude and prophecy of this sacred and universal concert of the nations. And secondly we may make this claim in memory of Bacon, the most illustrious chancellor of England, to whom we owe the first suggestion and opportunity for common counsel with regard to the universal reform of the sciences.

The College of Light was never founded. 'One unhappy day bringing tidings of massacre in Ireland and of outbreak of civil war there, confounded all plans for the whole winter'—thus Comenius described the frustration of his work. Civil war quickly diverted people's attention from the establishment of a great centre for scientific research on Baconian lines. With the consent of his English friends and patrons Comenius accepted an offer from Sweden and travelled there via Holland. A condition was added by the sponsors of his scheme 'that should God restore the peace, Comenius was not to refuse to return and take up his work'.

But he never came back to England. For several years he lived under Swedish protection in the city of Elbląg (Elbing) in Western

Prussia maintaining correspondence both with the Unity in Leszno and with his friends in London. After the abandonment of the Czech exiles by Swedish delegates at the peace conference in Westphalia he sought another patron who would both give him opportunity for work and be ready to espouse the Czech cause. In 1650, George of Rákoczy, the ruler of Transylvania, extended an invitation to Comenius and entrusted him with the reform of schools in his country. Comenius did not hesitate to accept an offer from the arch-enemy of the House of Hapsburg and spent on his territory (in Sáros Patak) several years. He returned to Leszno only after the outbreak of the Swedish-Polish war. During that struggle his house in Leszno was burnt to ashes and his precious library was destroyed. It was easier to exchange letters and ideas with Hartlib and other friends from a new home in Holland, than from war-torn Poland.

During the forties and fifties of the seventeenth century new books by Comenius usually found their way to England soon after publication, no matter where they appeared. The group of English educators and scholars who were interested in his ideas, and eagerly awaited the fruits of his pansophical studies, was growing steadily during his wandering in Central Europe. Only in the late fifties and in the sixties of the seventeenth century sceptical voices were heard in England. Doubts gained ground that the lofty scheme might never become a reality. Even Samuel Hartlib complained of the constant delays and Comenius' enforced occupation with less important projects. In September 1661 Hartlib wrote to John Winthrop, Governor of Connecticut, as follows: 'Mr Comenius is continually diverted by particular controversies of Socinians and others from his main Pansophical work but some weeks agoe hee wrote that hee would no more engage himself in any particular controversy but would refer them all to his pansophical worke.' This promise was not fulfilled.

In the meantime some friends of Hartlib and certain other scholars who were interested in the progress of natural knowledge were holding sessions in London and in Oxford. The outcome of their discussions, which began in 1649, was the foundation of the Royal Society of London in 1662. Out of the magnificent edifice of the College of Light a part at least was built by the more realistic English scientists. Comenius received the news concerning the founding and development of the Society without jealousy or bitterness. When in 1668 he eventually published his 'Via lucis' he dedicated it 'to the torch bearers of this enlightened age, the Fellows of the Royal Society of London, now bringing real philosophy to a happy birth'. In the preface he welcomed the new body, hoping that they would succeed in realizing their programme. 'We have no envy towards you; rather we congratulate you and applaud you and assure you of the applause of mankind. Throughout the world the news will be trumpeted that you are engaged in labours the purpose of which is to secure that human knowledge and the empire of the human mind over matter shall not for ever continue to be a feeble and uncertain thing.'

In the sixties of the seventeenth century Comenius was less interested in the theoretical part of his pansophy than in the programme for the pacification of the world and the renaissance of human society. In his efforts to reform the conditions of the world, and to achieve the unity of Christian civilization, he was more and more inspired by visions and prophecies, thus leaving the solid ground of scientific research. He was also more concerned with the fate of his people and of the Unity and wished to preserve its memory among the nations of the world. In 1660 he wrote a concise account of the rules by which the Unity was governed, 'Ratio ordinis et disciplinae'. It appeared in English in 1661, in two parts. The first was 'An Exhortation of the Churches of Bohemia to the Church of England; Wherein is Set Forth the Good of Unity, Order, Discipline and Obedience in Churches of the Brethren of Bohemia'. The second part was entitled: 'A Description of the Order and Discipline Used in the Churches of Bohemia.'

Interest in Comenius' own pansophic plans was rapidly waning in England as well as in other parts of the world during the sixties of the seventeenth century. On the other hand his 'Exhortation' was warmly received. Several writers from the ranks of the clergy quoted from it in their treatises. During the discussions concerning Church government after the Restoration, voices were heard recommending an incorporation of some of the disciplinary regulations of the Unity into the new constitution of the Church of England. They remained in a minority, but the book of Comenius was not forgotten. In 1703 a book was published in Edinburgh with the title 'Primitive Church Government in the Practice of the Reformed Churches in Bohemia'. Added to it were some notes from Comenius' 'Ratio'. This evidenced the permanent interest of Scottish Protestants in the country of John Hus and of his follower Paul Kravar, whose memory had lived in Scotland since his martyr death at St Andrews in 1433.

Even the minor works of Comenius became popular in England during his lifetime. Samuel Pepys left a note in his diary that one day he entertained himself with the play of Comenius. He probably read one of the dramatic pieces which Comenius composed in Sáros Patak.

During all this time the 'Janua' retained its position in schools and families. New editions of that work kept on coming from printing presses in England and on the continent. Another introduction into the study of Latin, the 'Orbis pictus' ('The World in Pictures'), which in fact was a shortened, simplified and illustrated version of the 'Janua' after its first publication in 1658, went through numberless editions and won the attention of both parents and teachers. An English edition appeared in 1659 under the title: 'J. A. Comenius' Visible World'. On the title-page it was recommended as 'one of his best essays and the most suitable to children's capacities of any that he hath hitherto made'. Even during the seventeenth and eighteenth centuries the book retained its popularity all over the world. In England it went into twelve editions; the last of which appeared in London in 1777.

IV. KOMENSKÝ THE AMERICAN

The brave old man Johannes Amos Comenius, the fame of whose worth hath been trumpetted as far as more than three languages (whereof everyone is indebted unto his *Janua*) could carry it, was indeed agreed withal by our Mr Winthrop in his travels through the Low Countries, to come over into New England and illuminate this [i.e. Harvard] Colledge and country in the quality of a president. But the sollicitations of the Swedish Ambassador, diverting him another way, that incomparable Moravian became not an American.

Cotton Mather, 'Magnalia Christi Americana' (1702), IV, 128.

In the summer of 1637 John Harvard arrived in New England. Among the books which he brought from England and later bequeathed to the college in Cambridge, Massachusetts, was Anchoran's 'Porta linguarum'. Thus two years after the founding of the college its library owned the book which had carried Comenius' fame all over Europe.

Little is known concerning the curriculum at Harvard College in the early period of its existence. We may assume that from Comenius' 'Janua' many students learnt Latin, those especially who 'came to the university not with intention to make scholarship their profession but only to get such learning as may serve for delight and ornament'. Several copies of successive editions of the 'Janua' were bequeathed to American libraries either by Harvard men or their heirs. There is therefore plenty of evidence of the use of the 'Janua' as a text-book throughout the seventeenth century. It was introduced also into the Boston Latin School. One copy of the 'Janua' is particularly interesting, for it was owned by an Indian student Joel Jacoomis who studied at Harvard with his friend Caleb Cheeshahteaumuck in 1665, and from the 'Janua' acquired a knowledge of Latin. Comenius' 'Janua' circulated in New England in a large number of copies and enhanced its author's reputation on the western side of the Atlantic. It is also known that an introduction to physics by Comenius ('Physicae ad lumen divinum reformatae synopsis') found its way to Harvard College. A copy of that book had been in possession of John Barnard, who entered the Boston Latin School in 1689, and graduated from Harvard in 1700.

Not only the 'Janua' but also the pansophic ideas and educational method of Comenius attracted the attention of those interested in the progress of learning in New England. It is very likely that John Winthrop (1606–1676), son of the Governor of Massachusetts, met Comenius in London during his stay there in the winter of 1641–42, which coincided with Comenius' sojourn there. As S. E. Morison pointed out in his 'Founding of Harvard College', 'John Winthrop Jr. was asked by the first board of Overseers, when he went abroad, to invite some outstanding figure in education to be Master of Harvard College—someone whose name alone would advertise the College and attract more students from England.'

Not only John Winthrop Jr. but also some English divines who were interested in missionary work among the Indians in New England took into consideration Comenius' unusual qualities and encouraged him to the journey across the Ocean. It would not have been difficult to combine educational work at Harvard with missionary activities among the Indians and to promote intellectual life in New England in both ways. In the preface to 'Via lucis' Comenius stated that he came to London in September 1641 'on the advice of certain pious theologians and bishops (the occasion being the propagation of the Gospel unto the nations of the world and in particular the sowing thereof made then in New England)'. When the interest in the College of Light faded somewhat there was more ground for the hope that Comenius would consider seriously both Mr Winthrop's sounding and the advice of his friends from the ranks of the English clergy. There was indeed some reason to expect that the 'incomparable Moravian would become an American'.

But after long deliberation Comenius declined the offer. According to Cotton Mather, whose story contains some truth despite confusion with regard to the date and circumstances, 'the sollicitations of the Swedish Ambassador diverted Comenius another way'. The invitation from the Swedish government was, no doubt, more attractive than the prospect of a long journey to the other shore of the Atlantic. Swedish troops still stood in the field and Swedish statesmen were bound by solemn pledges to work for the restoration of Bohemian liberties. It would hardly have been advisable for Comenius to refuse his services to the country which sponsored the Czech cause, and he could hardly decline to strengthen the bond between Sweden and the groups of exiles from Bohemia and Moravia.

Though Comenius never set foot on American soil he certainly influenced by his writings intellectual life in New England. As Albert Matthews has written in his illuminating article 'Comenius and Harvard College', the scholars of New England were not content with merely buying the works of Comenius or with using them at school or college; they also studied them and quoted them in their own books. The efforts of Comenius to save the Unity and its main principles from oblivion were crowned with remarkable success. The account of the sufferings of the faithful Christians in Bohemia and Moravia, which had appeared originally in Czech, and in 1648 in Latin, was translated into English and published in London in 1650. Copies of 'The History of the Bohemian Persecution', describing the savagery of Imperial officials and soldiers in Bohemia and Moravia after the White Mountain, circulated also in New England. The book reminded people of the plight and sacrifices of the Czech people during the Thirty Years' War and kept alive the memory of their heroic struggle for religious freedom.

Of special interest for theologians and ministers of churches in New England was Comenius' description of the rules and discipline of the Unity. A prominent Independent (Congregational) minister, Increase Mather, who was active successively as pastor in Boston and as President of Harvard College, was responsible for its introduction into New England as well as for its popularity. In 1661 he sent from Europe a copy of Comenius' 'Ratio ordinis et disciplinae' to his father Richard. The latter supported his views in his 'Defence of the Answer' (1664) by references to Comenius' work and gave him publicity in learned circles in New England.

In the Mather family, which had given New England prominent ministers and prolific writers, Comenius' 'Ratio' was held in high esteem. Various writers of that name quoted from it in their treatises and kept the memory of the Unity alive on the other side of the Atlantic just as some English divines did in their own country. Increase Mather in 1700 enthusiastically mentioned the order of the Unity in his 'Order of the Gospel Professed and Practiced by the Churches of Christ in New England' and referred to Comenius' 'Ratio' in the text. Increase's eldest son, Cotton Mather, in his 'Faithful Account of the Discipline Professed and Practiced in the Churches of New England' (1726) 'imitated a little what was done in the "Ratio Disciplinae Fratrum Bohemorum", written by that incomparable Comenius'. Similarly Samuel Mather, in his 'Apology for the Liberties of the Churches in New England'

(1738), supported his argument by quotations from a large number of books dealing with the history and government of Protestant Churches in Europe—it goes without saying that Comenius' 'Ratio' supplied him with many examples and was mentioned several times. More than a century after the publication of Cotton Mather's 'Faithful Account', in 1829, an interesting book appeared in Portland, Maine, under the title 'Ratio disciplinae; or the Constitution of the Congregational Churches', in which T. C. Upham reprinted extracts with alterations from the 'Ratio disciplinae fratrum bohemorum' by Comenius, and from Cotton Mather's account.

V. KOMENSKÝ THE HUMANIST

It is the salvation of the whole world that we seek....
                    Comenius, 'Via lucis' ('The Way of Light').

In the last decade of his life Comenius was absorbed by polemics with opponents from the ranks of the Dutch clergy. The invectives of Samuel Desmarets (Maresius) surpassed in incisiveness and bias anything that had been published during the years of struggle. The life of Comenius was really 'going down in sorrows and his years in lamentations'. Bitter controversies were not the only source of unhappiness and anxiety. The pacification of Europe was delayed by new conflicts. The war between England and Holland shattered the exile's hope in an effective collaboration of Protestant nations which might have brought a readjustment of the harsh terms of the Peace of Westphalia concerning their co-religionists in the Hapsburg lands. From his study in Amsterdam Comenius sent a message to the representatives of the belligerent countries, assembled at Breda. The book was entitled 'Angelus pacis' ('The Angel of Peace') and urged the delegates to terminate hostilities and restore peaceful relations. New problems were appearing on the horizon in this last phase of Comenius' life. The venerable educator was overshadowed by his younger contemporaries, who rose to prominence as his prestige and influence declined.

But from an outstanding member of the younger generation of thinkers, G. W. Leibniz, came a prophecy which has been fulfilled in modern times. After a temporary eclipse of the fame of

Comenius, interest in his work rapidly increased during the nineteenth century. Men of good will from all parts of the world really united in the praise of the deeds, hopes and aspirations of the exiled bishop of the Unity. His books were studied and his ideas influenced modern educators. We may say with Nicholas Murray Butler that the great educational revival of the nineteenth century shed the light of scholarly investigation into all sorts of dark places so that Comenius is honoured 'wherever teachers gather together and wherever education is the theme'. Summarizing the indebtedness of modern education to Comenius Butler wrote as follows: 'The infant school or kindergarten, the education of girls, the incorporation of history and geography in the curriculum, the value of drawing and manual training, the fundamental importance of self-training, the physical and the ethical elements in education, and finally, that education is for all, and not for a favoured few only, were all articles in the creed of Comenius.'

The crisis through which the world has been passing since the outbreak of hostilities in 1914 has opened our eyes to those other aspects of Comenius' life and work which were corollary to his educational theory. We realize that he really sought not only a partial reform but the salvation of the whole world. Accounts of his life which do not pay sufficient attention to his desire to improve the lot of mankind and to heal the scars of the long war, overlook one of the most important and dynamic factors in his life. During the forty years of exile he analysed the causes of unrest in the world and in several writings drew up a programme for a renaissance of human society. He linked the Czech cause with the broad scheme of a general pacification of Europe. Thus he set the example for his spiritual heir T. G. Masaryk, whose work for the liberation of the Czechs and Slovaks cannot be dissociated from noble efforts to build up new Europe on the ruins of autocratic monarchies. Comenius' activities have also inspired the present struggle of the Czechs and Slovaks against the conqueror and temporary master of their country.

Comenius was not a statesman. Nor was diplomacy or strategy his concern or occupation. He was depressed by the current political ideas and their application. He wrote in the 'Via lucis' that 'the main political theories on which the present rulers of the world support themselves are treacherous quagmires and the real causes of the generally tottering and indeed collapsing condition of the world'. His proposals differed from the rigid clauses of diplomatic peacemakers. They were not dictated by narrow expediency but emanated from the heart of a leader of homeless exiles. Toward the end of his life his thought was almost deflected from normal channels by belief in prophecies and miracles.

The lofty vision of the golden age to come comforted him in the years of depression and gloom. He never gave up hope that one day he might be able to announce how in his judgement 'learning, religion and government may be brought to certain immutable principles or bases, to their best foundation, so that ignorance, uncertainty, discussions, the noise and the tumult of disputes, quarrels and wars shall cease throughout the world, and light, peace, and health return, and the golden age which has ever been longed for, the age of light and peace and religion may be brought to sight'.

In various ways and on various occasions Comenius proclaimed his belief that the peoples of Europe will find the way out of the labyrinth of passions and conflicting interests and that they will join hands in the reconstruction of the continent. He did not expect salvation from mere military victories or diplomatic negotiations. The real causes of trouble were to be discovered and eliminated by the combined efforts of statesmen and scholars as a preliminary to the peace conference. Once he quoted a saying that a contentious philosophy was the parent of a contentious theology and consequently of the series of conflicts and devastating wars. His desire for the restoration of order and of normal relations between European countries was genuine and deeply rooted in his heart. He worked for peace among free peoples, knowing well that harmony cannot be restored by force or compulsion. His programme was a just and durable peace based on Christian principles, and a universal education based on natural knowledge.

He did not labour in vain. His writings and ideas were a permanent source of inspiration not only for his countrymen but for the whole civilized world. As a true patriot he worked for the liberation of his people and as a beneficent scholar he stands among the greatest of the humanists.

Comenius, the English Revolution, and our Present Plight

By OSKAR KOKOSCHKA
Painter, Poet and Dramatist

The visit of Jan Amos Komenský (Comenius), the Czech humanist, to London in 1641 evokes our particular interest to-day because official voices are now encouraging the aim of re-making the foundations of the social order, just as they were on the eve of the English Civil War when the famous exile paid his visit to England.

Contemporary printed documents show that England was then in the main stream of democratic thought, shared in common with progressive continental thinkers. But English history during the following two centuries until the days of the popularization of the ideas of Evolution and Social Progress is a record of estrangement between this great nation and its own democratic tradition.

When Comenius left his exile in Holland, he came to London on the assumption that he had been summoned by command of Parliament. In fact, Samuel Hartlib, author of the socialist Utopia 'Macaria',[1] had brought a proposal before Parliament, possibly acting on behalf of a group of members of the House, to invite his friend. Comenius was world-famous after publishing his 'Janua linguarum' ('Gate of Languages'), and he planned now a 'Janua rerum' ('Gate of Things'), for which he hoped to have the scientific support of an international 'clearing-house of thought', about Nature. The bearing of Comenius' visit on the origins of the future Royal Society, as well as on the development of the 'Encyclopaedia Britannica', is well known.[2]

Although great interest in schemes suggesting that the State should support secular learning had been previously shown by Francis Bacon, the planning of a Pansophic College was largely the result of the inspiration and missionary zeal of this much-

---

[1] S. Hartlib, a refugee from Prussia and author of 'A Description of the famous Kingdome of Macaria; showing its excellent Government, etc.' (London, 1641).

[2] R. Fitzgibbon Young, 'Comenius in England' (Oxford, 1932), and S. S. Laurie, 'John Amos Comenius, Bishop of the Moravians; his life and educational works' (Cambridge, 1884).

travelled educationalist. What is less realized is that the implicit association of his plan for an international college of 'International Philosophy' with the international reform of schools has not even yet been brought about. Many members of the House of Commons then shared the belief of Hartlib that the larger part of the confiscated Church funds would be devoted to educational purposes. What Comenius expected from his 'Pansophic College', as he told his patrons on his arrival, was the provision of really good text-books for the schools:

> For I remarked that men commonly do not speak but babble; that is, they transmit not as from mind to mind things on the sense of things, but exchange between themselves words not understood or little and ill understood. And that not only the common folk do this but even the half-educated also, and what is more to be grieved at, the well-educated themselves for the most part;...for which reason whatever language a man may speak, whether rude or cultured, it maketh slight difference since we are all nought but sounding brass and tinkling cymbals so long as *words*, not *things*—(the husks of *words*, I say, not the kernels of *meanings*)—be in our minds. Such a book, said I, could it be constructed aright, would be a kind of antidote-universal to ignorance, misunderstandings, hallucinations and errors. (Such were my hopes.) Yea, to the stinting of that complaint sometimes heard abroad that of the necessaries we are ignorant because the necessaries we learn not.

Comenius spoke little English, but in the England of his day he was understood in a literal and sympathetic sense. It was not a time of self-sufficient nationalism or mental inbreeding. In England there was at that time no fear of foreign ideas. There were philanthropists interested in Comenius who took at once to his educational views. To them he said: 'The Jesuits by their taking the schools have become the masters of the world, though they have nothing to compare with that of my community.' And there were refugees around Comenius, mostly Germans, fleeing from religious persecution and reminding the English people of the religion of the common people. Mystical strains, like those of the Lollards of the fourteenth century, and of the priests and friars, such as John Ball, who had thrown in their lot with the peasants, awoke again in the social unrest. The social discontent, though taking different forms in different countries, was international in its fundamental basis. It was the fight against feudalism, which was to find its highest expression in England during the years following Comenius' visit to London. Although arguments of an unmistakable, if crude, scientific materialism were already heard, most of his contemporaries believed with Comenius in religion as revealed to all human beings, the consequence of which is the essential equality of men. The existing order, outlasting its time, had come into opposition, in Protestant and Catholic countries alike, with this Christian principle of the human dignity of the individual.

As a politician Comenius shared with the masses the same desperate insistence on the imminence of a millennium of messianic deliverance from the sufferings due to the earthly rule of human authorities. Salvation is at hand—through education, thought Comenius. The whole continent was swept by insurrections against the continuance of serfdom, a movement yet to express itself in so decisive a way in England.

In the short confines of this contribution it would be difficult to produce convincing evidence in support of the statement that Peter of Chelcić, born in 1390, a Czech, was better suited to voice the meaning of the Reformation than the great Wyclif, Hus, Luther, Calvin or others, although he himself remained within the Catholic Church. Chelčický towards the end of his life formed a small lay community known as the Brethren of Chelcić, where persecuted Waldensians from Austria, with their old reformist tradition of an evangelical life in opposition to the Italian Church of the twelfth century, had found asylum. This community had with time developed into the Moravian or Bohemian Brethren, as a delegate of which Comenius came to England. 'A good Christian', wrote Chelčický in the 'Net of the True Faith', 'a follower of Christ, would not dare to allow himself to become King or Judge or Priest, ruling in a pagan rule over the people whom Christ alone ruleth.'

The revivification of the gospel ideas on equality was bound to bring despair to the guardians of law and order who saw the docility of the people endangered by this doctrine. Independently the learned Grotius had shortly before, in the Low Countries, brought back to men's minds the idea of Natural Law. It assisted in fashioning such claims as those put forward by the radical leaders of the English Revolution. But once the English Civil War had started on its course, there were many who thought it was going too far. 'Take away the declared, unrepealed law and then where is Meum and Tuum and Libertie and Propertie?'; that was what the more conservative Puritans began to ask themselves. Law must indeed conform to reason, but if dictated only by reason, it can degenerate into an expedient; as, for example, in the case of the wealthy Puritan traders who slowly got the better of their Dutch competitors in the slave trade, '...it being the birthright of every man to be alike free to transport that or any commodity into what part beyond the seas seemeth most advantageous to him'.

Richard Overton, one of the first English free-thinkers,[1] a friend of Comenius, in full political maturity, drove home the argument, decisive in a matter of rational persuasion:

Such hath been the misterious subtility from generation to generation of those cunning usurpers whereby they have driven on their wicked designes of tyranny and arbitrary domination under the fair, specious, deceitful pretences of Liberty and Freedom that the poore deceived people are even—in a manner—bestiallised in their understandings, become so stupid and grossly ignorant of themselves and of their own natural immunities and strength wherewith God by nature hath enriched them, that they are even degenerated from being men....

Unfortunately there were few people like Overton (who was imprisoned by Cromwell and again after the Restoration) prepared to say openly that rulers 'being lifted beyond their ordinary spheare of servants seek to become masters and degenerate into tyrants'.

How the merchants and tradesmen of the City, who beheaded an absolutist King and expropriated an intolerant Church, themselves came to exercise ecclesiastical and worldly tyranny, while depopulating the land by 'Enclosures' and bequeathing slums to

---

[1] His 'Man's Mortalitie' was published in 1643.

posterity, is too long a story to give here.[1] While the radical movement besieged the Long Parliament with petitions, Cromwell and Ireton went a long way with the men who were democratic in outlook and programme, but in the end the Lord Protector became the guardian of 'the order of property'. The army which demanded the completion of the social and political programme of the Revolution and for this purpose organized the democratic 'Council of the Army' (1647–49), was sent to fight in Ireland, where many of them settled down or perished, and thus were rendered impotent. The reformed victorious army came back to England, where the power of the sword took the place of all rational persuasion.

The tragic irony of it all is that without the support of the Puritan radicals with their high democratic hopes, such as Lilburne and Rainborough, Cromwell could not have fought the battles of the rising merchant middle class. The greatness of Comenius' ideas becomes more striking when one thinks how much more peaceful the development from feudalism towards the next stage of society—industrialism—might have been if the people of England had been allowed to reorganize themselves. Three centuries later the world still suffers misery and chaos because Comenius, the man with the message of universal brotherhood in knowledge and love, failed. Instead, a Cromwell is followed by a Wallenstein, a Frederick, a Bismarck, a Kaiser Wilhelm and even a Hitler.

In England the time was over for the rebels such as Winstanley,[2] who had dreamed of a mystical fraternity of mankind and of remaking order in social and economic equality according to the laws of reason. Salvation was coming only to the Chosen Elect of the Long Parliament, in whose aid Providence now sent the former Ironsides to prevent Enclosures being 'levelled' and new ditches 'digged' for Winstanley's co-operative farming. The Presbyterian aldermen of the City now preached that pauperism must be accepted as part of the divine order of Providence.

---

[1] Cf. G. P. Gooch, 'English Democratic Ideas in the Seventeenth Century' (London, 1927); E. Bernstein, 'Cromwell and Communism' (London, 1930); A. S. P. Woodhouse, 'Puritanism and Liberty' (London, 1938); H. Holorenshaw, 'The Levellers and the English Revolution' (London, 1939); D. W. Petegorsky, 'Left-wing Democracy in the English Civil War' (London, 1940).

[2] 'The Works of Gerrard Winstanley', ed. G. H. Sabine (Ithaca, N.Y. 1940).

Comenius left England on 21 June 1642, on the advice of his friend Hartlib.[1] Boarding his ship to Holland (Leyden)[2] he promised his English supporters that he would return when affairs in England were more propitious for his educational and scientific projects. But things fell out differently. Like Luther in Germany, Cromwell in England sent Democracy underground by advising his Puritan followers: 'You must cut these people' (the Levellers) 'in pieces or they will cut you in pieces.' On such principles future imperialism could develop and the iron rule of the Gentlemen of the City be enforced upon the mass of the people, upon the men, women and children, the landless proletariat, slaving in mills and later in coal mines, building up the future machinery of the industrial civilization.

Although his own life may have seemed to him a failure, Comenius was indeed one of those 'men of learning, *for the people*, furnished with ability in their several generations'.

Turning to our own situation in 1941, mass education seems sometimes to have been a failure. But Comenius' plan has not yet been realized. The resolve of the democratic peoples that this crusade against Fascism shall not again fade out in victory parades, but that it shall be succeeded by a long-lasting peace, can perhaps best be furthered by focusing attention on the problem of how to free the individual by removing the primary cause of his bondage, that is, education for national ends.

The armistice after the last 'war to end war' contained all the seeds of the next 'war to shape the world for good'. The League of Nations represented the governments and not the nations. The war had been fought to free oppressed minorities, but it was not thought necessary to free the majority from oppressive state-controlled educational systems.

With the break-up of the middle ages, nationalism rose to a position of dominance over all human affairs. Nationalism has made the tone of popular thought sometimes inhuman, sometimes superhuman, but never, properly speaking, normal and human.

---

[1] 'Samuel Hartlib; a sketch of his life and his relations to Comenius', by G. H. Turnbull (Oxford, 1920).

[2] 'Jean Amos Comenius, Sa vie et son œuvre d'éducateur', by Anna Heyberger (Paris, 1928).

We need a covenant on the guiding principles of rational education, in recognition of the fact that a mental world crisis underlies
the present series of homicidal world wars fought for 'holy causes'.
At the present time these reforms cannot be faced by a single
nation. The semi-religious worship of the dogma of national
sovereignty permeates education. Man cannot become conscious
of the possibilities of modern life if he is not aware of the fact that
the absurd state of world affairs, which makes his life futile, is not
caused by any nation singled out by its wickedness. Every international educationalists' congress, even in pre-Hitler Germany,
warned the governments that all the surgery of mass-massacres
had not healed the unemployment cancer, and that all the exacer-
bation of national rivalries by tariff barriers, curtailment of
freedom to travel, and hampering of mental cross-fertilization in
international human contacts, was only setting the stage for
another holocaust.

Modern industrial civilization necessitates that men of all
nations, peoples and colours must learn to live together and co-
operate or perish. State frontiers have become anomalies in an
age when an aeroplane crosses the Atlantic between breakfast and
dinner. But national-minded education still delivers its human
product ready rather to die for his dogmas than to criticize them
and live.

The atrocities of Fascist airmen at length taught the futility of
appeasement. Unfortunately the governments had seen to it that
the popular idea of collective security was strangled at the moment
of its birth. There was the isolationist policy: 'Fear God and keep
your powder dry'. There was the more business-minded policy
of Non-Intervention (of shameful memory) with its treatment of
Fascism as a heaven-sent cure for other people's discontents and a
bulwark against social change.

When the English-speaking peoples first heard the slogan 'Guns
instead of butter', they felt a Puritan shudder and believed that
Providence was marking out the 'Have-nots' to be given their
right deserts. But the defeated of the first world war were only the
first to give way to a spirit of recklessness. It was not long before
the new *national* economic theories, guiding post-war production

in contradiction to the needs of the consumer, and ignoring social necessities, had been adopted by the 'Haves' as well.

The first world war almost ruined the world. It cost the belligerents seventy thousand million pounds, although there were backward and depressed areas at home and elsewhere in which money might have been invested in a somewhat more productive way. But afterwards with the burning of food, with mass-unemployment and under-nutrition, with men not taught to do their jobs in society, nor to find or to offer jobs, the mental world crisis settled in for good. That total assault on civilization, of which Nazi-Fascism boasts to-day, could only have happened because modern man (like primitive man) tends to see things as notional, unreal, ghost-ridden. Even in the more advanced nations tests have shown that the average intelligence may not surpass that of an older child.

According to the statement of a leading English authority[1] on education, the majority of the electorate (which in democracy is decisive) 'suffers intellectual death' at the school-leaving age, which is about fourteen. Meanwhile in Germany, where under Hitler the standard of pre-war education was receding even from the meagre international committee's standard, the school-leaving age has been reduced to thirteen. After a long war, therefore, the future political decisions of a whole continent, if virtually controlled by Hitler, would have to be shaped by myths.

'To defend Democracy against Satan and Savagery' is well enough as a war slogan, if somewhat emotional and rhetorical. But in order to reach an intelligent decision on peace, man must have the intellectual equipment. Rationalism, accepted in theory by our technical civilization, compels democracy to look below the surface of things to find causes in accordance with natural law and with the facts of natural sciences. But so far, scientific truth, in the national state, has been but half-truth, like religious truth when the Church ruled human affairs.

Meanwhile our world is knocked to pieces by technical apparatus out of control. Democracy underrates the growing complacency

[1] Sir Richard Livingstone, 'The Future in Education' (Cambridge University Press, 1940), p. 4.

and despair of the backward masses, on both sides of the barricade, about the state of world affairs. If all the thinking is to be left to 'the authorities', the people would not need to be taught even the three R's. To-day we need more than ever the faith of Comenius in the talents latent in man. The essential principle of his educational plan translated into modern language demands from World Democracy an international scientific control of mass-education by a board of internationally minded educational experts and scientists. Such was the plea Jan Amos Comenius addressed to the Conference of Breda (1667) when the ideological wars of his time were ending. Three hundred years later Democracy has before it the opportunity to set up a World Education Board for the control of schools apart from any military settlements that may be made.

Such a World Board of scholars, scientists, and educational experts should be permeated by a spirit of federation like the mediaeval crafts, or 'mysteries'. It could not therefore be placed under the control of the functionaries of any single national state but should have independent self-jurisdiction as a body responsible for the development of all international cultural intercourse for peaceful purposes on the principles of mutual aid. Thus its academic ranks would be conferred according to internationally recognised scientific standards. Its assemblies would be formally recognised by international law. It would see that history was taught in such a way as to bring out the contributions which all peoples have made to human progress, and that science was taught in relation to its social relevance. Whereas Fascism or semi-religious Nationalism opens no new issues to mankind, a World Education Board, partaking even something of the nature of a sovereign body, would be the greatest instrument ever forged in the interest of world democracy, and thus indeed a realisation of Komenský's highest aims.

Comenius and Confidence in the Rational Mind

By DOROTHEA WALEY SINGER

Executive member of the Comité International de l'Histoire des Sciences

The recent commemoration of Comenius in Cambridge was an occasion fraught with significance greater even than that of the great man round whom the thoughts of those present gathered. We remembered his urgent message to humanity—a message still incompletely learned—his sufferings, typical of those endured by his fellow-countrymen through successive centuries, his life of wanderings in which he yet brought to expression those great thoughts which sound their urgent call around the whole globe and up to this very day—through space and time. How often has mankind been brought to the brink of a great reform and then failed to make good the clean leap forward. Yet the story of every great thinker reminds us that no mental effort is wasted. Wyclif retires to the country. John Hus is burned at the stake. Comenius wanders from land to land. Their message travels on.

Comenius gives the impression of a most modest, pious soul. Yet he is conscious that the task is laid on him:

O learned scholars, I beseech you not to despise these suggestions because they originate with one less learned than yourselves. Remember the saying of Chrysippus 'many a market gardener has spoken to the point. Perchance an ass may know what you do not....' It is the love of God and the wish to improve the condition of humanity that goads me on and will not suffer me to keep silence when my instinct tells me what should be done.

Or again:

It is a law of human existence that if any know of assistance lying close at hand to those who are struggling he should not withhold it; especially in a place, as in the one before us, where the matter concerns not one but many, and not individuals merely but towns, provinces, kingdoms, the whole human race.

The assistance that he would give is no less than a universal and reformed system of education:

In every well-ordered habitation of man (whether city, town, or village), a school or place of education for the young should be erected.... Not the children of the rich or of the powerful only, but of all alike, boys and girls, both noble and simple, rich and poor, in all cities and towns, villages and hamlets, should be sent to school.

Comenius is determined that the road of knowledge shall be made pleasant for the child. He promises a book of hints for mothers and nurses and he published a picture book for children, the 'Orbis sensualium pictus'. But it is not merely a general benevolence that dictates his revolt against the dull and inefficient teaching of children:

It is to the advantage of heaven that schools should be reformed for the exact and universal culture of the intellect.

Until very recent years it would have seemed a truism to epitomize the course of human history as a persistent effort to use and develop Mind and Reason. Passing those earliest centuries in East and West of which we are gradually beginning to get some comprehension, and coming to our own continent and our modern epoch, we see Comenius as part of the great Renaissance insurgence of belief in the human Intellect, directing human Will.

The message can, of course, be traced back to the leaders of thought in many lands, but the lead to the men of the Renaissance came from Italy. Petrarch (1304-74), 'On a remedy for either fortune'; Manetti, 'On the Dignity and Excellence of Man' (1436); contrasted the created and completed World of Nature with the ever-developing world of human culture. Pico della Mirandola (1463-94) had the same conception. In Nicholas of Cusa in the Rhineland (1401-64) the thought is bound up with his idea, derived from the Spanish Moslem, Averroes (1126-98), of an inter-related Universe and of Man as part of Universal Mind. Ficino (1433-99) expounds the same theme. Most finely it was expressed by Giordano Bruno (1546-1600) in that brief interlude when he, a wandering exile like Comenius after him, was rejoicing in intellectual commerce with a happy band of adventurous thinkers in London:

The Universal Intellect is the most real and powerful part of the soul of the world. This is a single whole which fills the whole, illumines the universe and directs nature to the production of suitable species: this is concerned with the production of natural things as our intellect with the (fitting) congruous production of rational kinds. This is called by the Pythagoreans the Motive Force and mover of the universe, as said the poet:

'Mind moveth the whole form and is poured into the limbs and mixeth itself throughout the body.'

The tale is taken up by Descartes (1596–1650): *Cogito, ergo sum.* Spinoza (1632–77), contemporary of Comenius, urging Man to use his Reason, has to lament:

The natural light is not so much despised as cursed by many, as the source of impiety.

Spinoza also pointed out that our method of thought is part of the vast realm of Nature of which we must seek to understand the laws. Kant and the philosophers who succeeded him have the vision of Man's progress by virtue of Mind.

The 'Natural Philosophers' pursued the same theme. To understand Natural Law is for them the supreme task of the human intellect. Newton (1642–1727), in his Preface to the 'Principia', admonishing his readers of the importance of the art of Geometry and warning them that 'Errors are not of the Art but of the Artificers' continues 'but we, consulting not the Arts but Philosophy, write not by manual powers but by those inherent in our nature'. Quotations could of course be multiplied from the great explorers of Nature throughout the eighteenth and nineteenth centuries.

Even a generation ago, it would have seemed trite to offer these examples of Man's confidence in his own Mind. But there came that cloud, no bigger than a man's hand, portent of perhaps the most terrible storm that has assailed the mental life of mankind.

The successive works of William James (1842–1910) and his 'pragmatic' disciples, the rapier-like intellect of Bergson summoning men to the worship of a cloudy 'Evolution Créatrice' (1907), the sad pessimism of Thomas Hardy culminating in the irrational prophecies of some contemporary physicists, the intuitionism of writers such as D. H. Lawrence, the mystical racialism of a Gobineau and his followers, the 'modern myths' of a Rosenberg, the highly organized wickedness of a Hitler—in all these we can see a certain relation and succession. But fortunately there is also the succession of those who, firmly opposing these writers, have witnessed to the value of the free Mind and Reason, so terribly assailed during these years, yet valiantly battling for human goodness, human happiness, for humanity itself. Vernon Lee's 'Vital Lies', Julien Benda's 'La Trahison des Clercs', the great architects of the philosophies of Emergent Evolution, of Holism, the magnificent and fearless mind of James' great successor at Harvard, and most recently the author of that poetic biological masterpiece 'Man on his Nature'; these and many others have been and are showing the way to our own generation for the restoration of Man's faith in the cultivation of his special gift of Mind. Thus the message of Comenius is carried forward to generations unborn.

Let us say with him:

Ye men of learning, to whom God has given wisdom and keen judgement that ye may be able to criticise such matters as these and improve them by your counsels, see that ye delay not to assist the sacred fire with your sparks, nay, rather with your torches and with your fans.

The Social Relations of Science in the seventeenth and the twentieth centuries

By J. G. CROWTHER

Scientific Correspondent of the Manchester Guardian

In his 'Great Didactic', published in 1657, five years before the incorporation of the Royal Society, Comenius proposed the foundation of a Universal College whose members 'should make it the object of their combined labours to establish thoroughly the foundations of the sciences, to spread the light of wisdom throughout the human race with greater success than has heretofore been attained, and to benefit mankind by new and useful inventions'.

The social importance of science, as a means for bettering the condition of mankind, was thus keenly appreciated by Comenius, and other great thinkers of the seventeenth century. They expressed a widely held belief, which led to the foundation of the Royal Society, and the writing of such remarkable books as those of Thomas Sprat,[1] on the history of the origin and activities of that Society during the first five years of its existence, and Joseph Glanvill,[2] whose brisk attack on the decaying Aristotelian philosophy cleared the way for the Society's work.

The enthusiasm in the possibilities of science shown by Comenius, Bacon, Sprat, and other men of their time, did not persist very long. It had declined by the beginning of the eighteenth century. The period of illimitable speculation seemed to be followed by a drearier period of modest practical achievements. One way of expressing the change is to say that the scientists were ceasing to dream, and were getting down to work. When men like Boyle, Hooke and Newton were beginning to get actual results, there was a revulsion against speculation, and any new fact, however trivial, became more esteemed than the grandest hopes of human betterment by scientific discovery. The point of view which has been classical for the last two hundred and fifty years was established.

---

[1] 'History of the Royal Society of London', by Thomas Sprat (1667).
[2] 'Scepsis Scientifica', by Joseph Glanvill (1661; repr. 1885), and 'Plus ultra' (1668).

The discovery of new scientific facts entirely for their own sake has been the tradition.

To-day there is a growth of interest in science as an instrument which affects the destiny of mankind. This is distinct from the tradition dating from the time of Newton, and resembles rather that of Bacon, Comenius and Sprat.

Why should the twentieth century see an enthusiasm for the social relations of science, which resembles that of the seventeenth century, and differs from the attitude towards science in the two intervening centuries? The answer that immediately suggests itself is that there are similarities in the underlying conditions in the seventeenth and the twentieth centuries. The seventeenth century was a period of exceptionally intense strife in religion, war and industry. The Thirty Years' War and the Civil War in England are remembered well enough. The degree of industrial change and struggle has been appreciated only recently. Nef and other scholars have shown that the burst of scientific discovery accompanying the foundation of the Royal Society occurred in parallel with a great industrial revolution. The speed of development of the English industrial revolution of the seventeenth century was even faster than that of the development of industry in the first half of the eighteenth century.

The decline of enthusiasm in the possibilities of science noticeable at the beginning of the eighteenth century occurred when the parallel economic development began to slow down. G. N. Clark has suggested that one of the causes in this decline in the speed of development of science and industry is connected with the development of trade with India and the East. The new sea trade with the Orient brought high profits without the use of inventive ingenuity, and capital could be accumulated without improving industrial processes. If the conditions of life were improving without science, why be enthusiastic about it?

Under these conditions, research becomes the satisfaction of the curiosity, and the amusement, of wealthy gentlemen. The pre-occupation of a Newton with the technicalities of a problem fit in with the desires of the wealthy curious. Enthusiasm for science as a means for the betterment of mankind declines.

The situation changed in the latter half of the century. The emphasis on science as an aid to industry became stronger. The industrialists in Scotland, the Midlands and the North encouraged scientists to improve their processes, or became scientists themselves for this end. There was a renewed enthusiasm for science, but different in nature from that of the seventeenth century. Science was to be cultivated for the benefit of mankind, but through industry as the intermediary. The idea of utilizing science directly for the benefit of mankind had receded.

The successful growth of capitalist industry since the eighteenth century has provided a steady foundation for this conception, and has made it classical during the succeeding period. The changes and difficulties of the present time have undermined this conception of science. Capitalist enterprise can no longer be regarded as the best medium for giving the benefits of science to mankind. The old mechanism for utilizing science has broken down. The event has impressed on many, for the first time, that some kind of social mechanism is necessary to enjoy the fruits of science. This has naturally promoted enquiries into the social relations of science, in order to discover which forms are possible, and which are best, as means of utilizing science for the benefit of mankind.

The present convulsions in human society contain ideological, military and economic elements that resemble those that dominated the convulsions of the seventeenth century. The enthusiasm in both centuries for the social possibilities of science has arisen from similar causes. The gifted men who met together in the seventeenth century to prosecute the advancement of science believed themselves to live in a miserable time. Sprat wrote that the founders of the Royal Society intended 'no more than only the satisfaction of breathing a free air, and of conversing in quiet one with another, without being ingag'd in the passions and madness of that dismal age'.

Their visions of the possibilities of science must have seemed idealistic dreams against the background of contemporary life. And yet Newton was already living among them, unsuspected. He entered into residence at Trinity College in Cambridge in 1661, the year before the Invisible College was incorporated as the Royal Society. The University was badly disorganized after twenty years of the Civil War. It had lost many of its best scholars and much of its funds. Students entering the University to-day may remember that Newton also studied under difficult conditions, which might have made application seem unprofitable.

The passion for science as an aid for mankind was strong then, because social chaos forced men to strive for a rational or scientific way of life.

We, like Sprat and Newton, find ourselves living in a 'gloomy season'. Like the men of that century, we live with ideological struggles, wars, and a swift technological development. These may be a scourge, but if the experience of the seventeenth century is a guide, they may also be the opportunity for constructive enthusiasm. The interest in the social relations of science was the signal of activities which have given the seventeenth century the title of 'the century of genius'. May not the new interest in the social relations of science to-day be a signal of activities which will qualify the twentieth century to appropriate that title? The history of science gives some suggestions that we may approach the difficult future with particular confidence of success.

The Debt of Europe to Czechoslovakia and to Comenius

By ERNEST BARKER

*Emeritus Professor of Political Science in the
University of Cambridge*

If I may be romantic, I will begin in the garden of a shepherd's cottage, in 'a desert country near the sea', on the coast of Bohemia. One of Shakespeare's loveliest heroines—her name is Perdita, the lost one, but she is soon to be found and restored—is gathering flowers and sprigs in the garden. She brings them to Polixenes, the king of Bohemia—to-day we should call him President, and address him as Dr Beneš—and offering them to him and to his companion she says

> Reverend Sirs,
> For you there's rosemary and rue:...
> Grace and rememberance be to you both,
> And welcome.

We are here, Your Excellency, to offer 'grace and rememberance' to you both—to the country you represent and to one of its greatest sons, John Amos Comenius. But before I pass to the grave historic mood that suits my theme, may I continue to be romantic, and may I invoke the memory of two other heroines—heroines at any rate to me—who are, like Perdita, at any rate in my imagination, naturally present to-day, with their grace and benediction, at our ceremony of remembrance? One of the two is the good Queen Anne of Bohemia, daughter of the Czech-loving Emperor, Charles IV, who founded the University of Prague: wife, at the age of sixteen, of our King Richard II: the lady to whom Chaucer dedicated his 'Legend of Good Women': the lady whom Richard loved so deeply that he would never revisit, after her death, the manor of Sheen in which she had died: the lady after whose death he lost his bearings and, in a few years, his throne. By the side of the good Queen Anne, to whom religion always meant much, you may see two men of religion: grave John Wyclif of Oxford and grave John Hus of Prague, both masters of theology, both morning-stars of the Reformation. There is one heroine, and her

78

attendants, and there is also one theme—the theme of religion. The other heroine is a Stuart lady, Elizabeth, daughter of our King James I: married, also at the age of sixteen, to the Elector Frederic of the Palatinate: Queen of Bohemia, for a brief season, in the winter of 1619-20: a lady so charming that men called her Queen of Hearts, and enshrined her in their poems: a lady so vexed by tribulations in the wars of religion, that she was long remembered, in our national memory, as a martyr to Protestantism: a lady of romance and tragedy, whose body lies, like that of the good Queen Anne, in Westminster Abbey, and who was the ancestress, through her daughter Sophia, of our present Kings. In her life, too, religion meant much. By her side, too, there stands the figure of a man—not that, I imagine, they ever met or were ever connected: but they were almost exact contemporaries, both born in the nineties of the sixteenth century, within a few years of one another, and both dying early in the second half of the seventeenth. The man is Comenius, Presiding Bishop, in his later years, of the religious society called the Bohemian Brethren, or the Unitas Fratrum, but known to us mainly to-day as a man of education, and celebrated among us for his 'Great Didactic' and the many contributions he made to the general advancement of learning, science and education.

There emerges from this prelude—or there is meant to emerge; for I may not have succeeded in striking the notes firmly enough to make them audible—a double motif; or perhaps I had better say a single motif which has two sides or manifestations. It is the motif of religion and education. In a word, I should say that the debt of Europe to Czechoslovakia is primarily and mainly a debt in the sphere of religion, which is also—already in the fourteenth century and in the early history of the University of Prague, but more especially in the seventeenth century and the history of the influence of Comenius—a debt in the sphere of education. The two things go together, and cannot be divided in the history of the Czechoslovak genius—religion and education: education and religion.

This is how I look at the matter. Somewhere in the middle of the fifth century of our era, about the time of the fall of the Western

Roman Empire, the Czechs entered Bohemia, that nuclear and focal region of Europe. For nearly a thousand years they grew and matured, quietly and generally unnoticed; and then, towards the middle of the fourteenth century, under the reign of that brilliant and remarkable House of Luxemburg to which Charles IV belonged, they flowered. They had developed a subtle and musical language—a language unknown to me, so that I only speak from hearsay, but I shall venture to affirm, trusting to good hearsay, a language issuing naturally in song and music, and belonging naturally to the genius of a musical people. But the Czechs were not content to link language only with music. They linked it also with thought, education, and the expression of religious feeling and religious speculation. The University of Prague was like an Athena, springing fully armed into life; and in the latter half of the fourteenth century, around the University, there was a flowering of the Czech language, Czech literature, and the Czech soul. A gifted people found itself: it discovered and expressed to Europe —and I might almost say that it was the first of European peoples to do so—a national consciousness. But Czech nationalism—if I may use that word of a period that was still in the middle ages— was not a secular nationalism. It was a religious nationalism; and that to me is its greatness and its native nobility. The Czechs sought to find themselves by finding their own way of religious life—escaping from alien elements and the trammels of orthodox formalism into the freedom of a native religious movement true to their own inner sense. We in this country may have been of some help to them in their strivings. 'From Oxford', as one of our bishops has written, 'the writings of Wyclif were brought to Prague, as early as 1385, by Jerome of Prague, who was himself a student of Oxford'. But whatever we English may have given, the movement of Czech religious nationalism, led by Hus, was essentially Czech and essentially native. What a stirring and tragic and glorious movement it was, as it fought its way, first by the word, and then, under the great Ziska and his successor Prokop, by the sword! The Puritans of Central Europe, two centuries before our Puritans, with their own New Model Army two centuries before our New Model and the days of our Oliver Cromwell—such were the fiery and stormy Hussites, of the early decades of the fifteenth century. And if their movement died down, after the battle of Lipan in 1434, and seemed as if it had been a great and fitful fever, it still left an inheritance to Europe. Some of the seeds of the European Reformation were seeds which came from the sowing of the Czechs. Zwingli read Hus and learned from Hus; Luther too, as early as 1508, was reading the works of Hus in his monastery at Erfurt; and when he translated the Latin Vulgate into the vernacular, he was doing again what the Czech Hussites, like our English Lollards, had already done before.

Twice in European history—twice, that is to say, before those sombre and unforgettable days of September and October 1938—the Czechs were drawn into the foreground of European affairs. The second occasion, after the Hussite Wars of the early fifteenth century, was the beginning of the Thirty Years' War, early in the seventeenth century. Once more a mixed movement—partly religious and Protestant, partly national and constitutional—surged into being; the Czech Protestant nobility rose against a Catholic and absolutist Hapsburg; and their rising began a war, destined to vex Europe for thirty years, in the course of which, as I have already had reason to note, our Stuart Princess Elizabeth was drawn to Prague and its fortunes. Alas, so far as the Czechs were concerned, fortune was swiftly and peremptorily cruel. On a November day in 1620 the battle of the White Mountain was fought and lost just outside the walls of Prague. The result was heavy for the Czechs. Deprived of a native nobility, they were reduced, for centuries to come, to the status of a peasant people. They went back into the desert, to repair their strength in quiet with a patient fortitude. But one thing, and one influence, still survived, and continued to survive, in Europe. This was the Unitas Fratrum, the Bohemian Brethren, or, as it later became, in the course of the eighteenth century, 'the Unity of Moravian Brethren'. Let me say some words on this theme. It will lead directly to Comenius and to the end of my discourse.

So far as I know—but my knowledge is not magisterial—the Bohemian Brethren go back to the Hussites and are as old as the fifteenth century. Their history is a continuous thread—a European thread—which runs from John Hus to John Wesley, and even to the present day, and joins in its course Czechoslovakia to Poland, to Hungary, to Saxony, to England, and to the United States. I cannot but celebrate its first figure, Peter Chelčický, a Tolstoi before Tolstoi and a Quaker before George Fox, the leader of the advanced reforming party among the Hussites in the latter half of the fifteenth century. By himself, he might have led the brethren whom he founded into a desert of millenniarism; but the Unitas Fratrum (Jednota Bratrska), with the steady and solid sense inherent in the Czechs, and with a Czech gift for order and organization, settled down into a middle way which reconciled the aspirations of millenniarism with the needs of modernism. They became an episcopally organized Church, which based itself directly on the Bible: they emphasized conduct as well as creed: they had a discipline (did not Comenius, one of their later bishops, write a 'Ratio disciplinae'?) which divided adherents into Perfect, Proficient and Beginners. They had also a passion for education: they were early and busy users of the printing press: they had printed a hymn-book by 1501, and by 1593 they had their version of the whole Bible, the Kralice Bible, in Czech. They cherished and developed the mother tongue: they studied educational methods: they pursued researches in history, language, and eventually science.

This, you will see, is the rock from which Comenius was hewn; but before I turn to him I desire to say a further word about the Bohemian Brethren. Already, as early as 1547, they had suffered persecution, and some had settled in Poland and founded churches and schools; but they still survived in their own country, where they included many of the nobles among their adherents. The defeat of the White Mountain in 1620 was fatal to their continuance in their own country. They were scattered: they went, as Comenius says, 'into neighbouring districts of Germany, and a great part of us also into Poland and Hungary'. Comenius went into Poland: he settled at Leszno, where there had been a community since 1548: he became a bishop of the Church of the Brethren in 1632, holding it together and seeking to comfort and help 'the Hidden Seed' which remained in Czechoslovakia. That seed, as I must now mention, was destined to a curious history. It largely migrated, about 1720, into Saxony, under the patronage of a Lutheran Pietist called Count Zinzendorf; it passed, through its contact with Lutheranism, into a Moravian Church, styled by the name of 'the Unity of Moravian Brethren'. Thus the Bohemian Brethren, transmigrated in Germany, and receiving a tincture of German Lutheranism, passed into the Moravian Brethren; and these Moravian Brethren not only settled in England (where they had something to do with the early religious experiences of John Wesley, and where they were recognized in 1749 by our Parliament as 'an ancient Protestant episcopal church'), but also, across the Atlantic, in Georgia and (I think) Carolina. Not only Europe, but also America, owes an ultimate debt to the Bohemian Brethren.

Comenius is the finest expression, but he is an extension as well as an expression, of the native and original genius of the Bohemian Brethren. He is also, by virtue of that fact, an expression of the devotion of the Czech people to the mixed and kindred causes of religion and education. He is an epitome of everything I have been trying to suggest in my address. I cannot better describe him than in the words of a Czech colleague, a professor in a new Czech University which is called the Masaryk University. 'He was a devout Christian and a loyal Czech, as well as an ardent Pansophist and the forerunner of the Encyclopaedists.' I see Comenius by the side of Masaryk; and I see Masaryk by the side of Comenius. The debt of Europe to Czechoslovakia is mirrored and reflected in the debt of Europe to Comenius.

Exiled from his country in 1628, at the age of thirty-six, he spent the next forty-two years of his life in the service of religion and sound education throughout the length and breadth of Europe. He served in Poland: he served in England, which he visited just before our Civil War, three hundred years ago; he served in Sweden, where he laboured under Oxenstierna; he visited Hungary: he also served in Holland, where he published the last of his books, and where he died. He is remembered among us to-day as a great figure in the history of education—the author of the 'Great Didactic': a pioneer in the teaching of modern languages; one of the earliest advocates, if not the earliest, of universal and compulsory elementary education; a pioneer, in the spirit of Bacon, of the encyclopaedic development of science and of the foundation of scientific colleges or societies, such as our Royal Society, as instruments of that development. He deserves all 'the grace and rememberance' which he receives in our Universities, and especially in our University departments of education; but I think he deserves even more. The cause of education was linked in his mind—as it has been generally linked through the centuries in the aspirations of the Czech genius which he so largely embodied—with the cause of religion. He was the bishop of the Bohemian Brethren as well as the author of the 'Great Didactic'; and he was both in one. We see both trends converging in his plans for the spread of learning and the spread of religious missions among the Indians of America. That brings me to one of the last works Comenius wrote, and with it to the end of my discourse.

In 1667, at the age of seventy-five, he published at Amsterdam his 'Angelus pacis'—'the Angel of Peace'. It was a plea for a peace league of European states—for he too, as other great Czechs have been in our day, was a labourer in the cause of a League of Nations. My friend Dr R. F. Young, in a work of rare learning on "Comenius in England", has quoted a passage from the 'Angelus pacis'. It is an appeal to the European nations to bring 'the many barbarous uneducated peoples with whom we trade' to the true faith and to education. 'This', he says, 'the English happily began a few years ago in New England, but the other nations have up to the present paid much less attention to the matter'. That is a tribute of which we may be proud. Comenius gave us a garland. He deserves any garland we can give him to-day—to-day, just three hundred years, exactly three hundred years, from the time of the autumn equinox, when, summoned by friends who were in touch with our Long Parliament, he came to England, on 21 September 1641, to give what he could to our nation and to the cause of religion and education.

Note: The author, at the time of the delivery of this address, was moved to quote a story which he had just heard from the lips of Professor Seton Watson. He ventures to repeat it here. Towards the end of the last war, some time in 1918, a body of Czech soldiers were being shown round Winchester Cathedral. Their guide observed that, when they were being shown the tomb of Cardinal Beaufort, bishop of Winchester and papal legate in the fourth 'crusade' against the Hussites in 1427, the Czech soldiers drew together and whispered to one another. Then, when they had come out of the Cathedral, and were in the open, they lined up, and sang together a great Hussite song of the fifteenth century. What a historic memory; and what a people—true, after five hundred years, to its abiding tradition and its ancient faith!

Table of Dates

Illustrating the Life of Comenius (Komenský)

with special reference to his plans for pansophic encyclopaedias and scientific societies, and to his interest in educational work among the Indians of New England and Virginia.

By R. FITZGIBBON YOUNG

1592. Jan Amos Komenský (Comenius), born at Uherský Brod[1] in Eastern Moravia in the Kingdom of Bohemia. (J. V. Novák and J. Hendrich, 'J. A. Komenský' (1931), 1. 2.)

1608–11. Comenius studied at the Latin School maintained by the Unitas Fratrum (Bohemian Brethren) at Přerov in Moravia.

1611–13. Comenius at the University of Herborn in Nassau, where one of his teachers was J. A. Alstedt, who published in 1608 his 'Encyclopaedia cursus philosophici', expanded later into 'Encyclopaedia omnium scientiarum' (1630). These works and also Alstedt's 'Clavis artis Lullianae' (1633) had much influence on Comenius.

1613. Comenius at Heidelberg University.

1614–27. Comenius composed his *Theatrum universitatis rerum* in MS. It contains the germ of his pansophic ideas.

1616. Comenius ordained deacon and priest of the Unitas Fratrum at Žeravice in Moravia.

1620–28. After the victory of the Imperialists at the White Mountain on 8 November 1620 the Emperor Ferdinand II adopted a series of repressive measures against all the non-Catholic cults in Bohemia and Moravia except Judaism. (See R. F. Young, 'Comenius in England', p. 26.)

1628. Comenius left Bohemia and went into exile at Leszno in Poland, where he taught in the College belonging to the Unitas Fratrum. (See 'Comenius in England', p. 26.)

1628–32. Comenius composed his *Didactica* in Czech. The original Czech MS. is now in the National Museum at Prague. The Czech text was published at Prague in 1849. An expanded Latin version was published at Amsterdam in 1657 under the title *Didactica magna* in *Opera didactica omnia*, 1. 196.

---

[1] Komna and Nivnice are villages near Uherský Brod; Komenský had family connections with all these and the first two have also each been claimed as his birth-place, but the bulk of evidence indicates the third.

1631. *Janua linguarum reserata* published at Leszno. It is a grammar in the form of a miniature compendium of useful knowledge. It had an enormous circulation. (See 'Comenius in England', pp. 27–8.) A pirated edition by Anchoran was published in London in 1632. *The Labyrinth of the World* (*Labyrint světa*) published in Czech at Leszno. *Informatorium Škole Materské* published at Leszno. (See 'Comenius in England', p. 66.)

1632. Comenius consecrated a Bishop (Senior) of the Unitas Fratrum at Leszno.

1633. *Ratio disciplinae ordinisque ecclesiastici in Unitate Fratrum Bohemorum* published at Leszno.
Januae linguarum reseratae vestibulum published at Leszno. Preface dated 4 January 1633.

1633. *Physicae ad Lumen divinum reformatae Synopsis* published at Leipzig. It was translated into English in 1651 as *Naturall Philosophie*.

1635. *Leges illustris Gymnasii Lesnensis* drawn up by Comenius in MS. in 1635. *Januae linguarum reseratae vestibulum* republished at Leszno.

1633–38. *Didactica Magna* expanded in Latin from the Czech *Didactica*. (See 'Comenius in England', p. 29.)

1633. Comenius asked Count Raphael Leszczyński in October 1633 to finance his scheme for a pansophic encyclopaedia.

1636. Death of Count Raphael Leszczyński.

1637. *Conatuum Comenianorum praeludia ex Bibliotheca S. H.* published by Hartlib at Oxford. (See 'Comenius in England', p. 35.)
Comenius sent to Hartlib a MS. draft *De Pansophia* which is now in the Public Record Office in London. (See 'Comenius in England', p. 57.)

1638. *De sermonis Latini studio per vestibulum, januam, palatium, etc.*, published at Breslau. (See 'Comenius in England', p. 29.)
Conatuum pansophicorum dilucidatio, published at Leszno. (See *op. cit.* p. 69.)

1639. *Pansophiae Prodromus*, largely a reprint of the *Dilucidatio*, published by Hartlib in London.

1640. Comenius begged Count Bogusław Leszczyński to finance his pansophic encyclopaedia.
Comenius began to compose his *Janua rerum*.

1641–42. Komenský's visit to England (21 September 1641 to 21 June 1642), during which he wrote *Via lucis*, published in 1668.
Comenius was probably invited by the younger John Winthrop to visit New England. (R. F. Young, 'Comenius and the Indians of New England' (1929), pp. 1–4.)

1642. Hartlib published at London in January 1642 an English translation of *Conatuum pansophicorum dilucidatio* under the title *A Reformation of Schooles, etc.*

Comenius met Descartes at Endegeest, near Leiden, in October 1642. (See 'Comenius in England', p. 50.)

1643. *Pansophiae diatyposis* published at Danzig. It was translated into English by Jeremy Collier and published in London in 1652.

Comenius composed his *Consultatio catholica*, part of which was published in Amsterdam in 1662.

1646. *Tabula pansophica* published at Danzig.

1647. Comenius wrote to Hartlib on 5/15 June 1647, expressing his deep sympathy with the educational work that was being carried on among the Indians of New England and Virginia. (Patera, 'Korr. J. A. Komenského', No. 111, p. 134. Cf. R. F. Young, 'Comenius and the Indians of New England' (1929), pp. 17–18.)

Hartlib wrote to Comenius, urging him to translate his *Didactica* into English with a dedication to the Parliament. Patera, *op. cit.* p. 134.

1648. *Linguarum methodus novissima* published at Leszno.

Comenius appointed Presiding Bishop of the Unitas Fratrum on the death of Bishop Justinus.

1649. A small portion of *Janua rerum* published at Leszno. No copies are known to be extant. (Kvačala, 'Korr. J. A. Komenského', II, No. 241. See p. 49.) His *Janua rerum reserata* was published at Leiden in 1681, after his death.

1651. *Schola Pansophica* published at Saros Patak in Hungary.

1655. Komenský's letter of 24 May 1655 to Andrew Klobusický, referring to 'his class in America'. (Patera, 'Korr. J. A. Komenského', No. 111. See 'Comenius in England', pp. 61 and 93.)

1657. Comenius and his fellow exiles at Leszno invited by Oliver Cromwell to settle in Ireland. The offer was declined. (R. Vaughan, 'Protectorate of Oliver Cromwell', II. 447–9; Patera, 'Korr. J. A. Komenského', No. 176.)

Opera didactica omnia published at Amsterdam.

1658. *Orbis pictus* published at Nuremberg. This work, which was one of the first illustrated school text-books in Europe, is merely an expansion of *Janua linguarum reserata* (1631) with illustrations.

1659. *Cartesius cum sua naturali philosophia a mechanicis eversa* published at Amsterdam.

1660. *Ecclesiae Slavonicae...brevis historiola.* This little work was printed at Amsterdam as part of Komenský's *De bono unitatis et ordinis*, with a dedication to Charles II of England.

1667. *Angelus pacis*, published at Amsterdam. In this plea for a Peace League of European States, addressed to the English and Dutch envoys at the Conference of Breda in May 1667, Comenius urges in chapter 44 that the European nations should bring 'the many barbarous uneducated peoples with whom we trade in the two Indies' to the true faith and to education in morals and the sciences. 'This the English happily began a few years ago in New England.' (See 'Comenius in England', p. 61.)

1668. *Via lucis*, published at Amsterdam with a dedication to the Royal Society, begging them not to neglect metaphysics. (See 'Comenius in England', p. 44.)

1669. Komenský's tractate *De Zelo sine scientia*, addressed to Dr Samuel Desmarets of Groningen, published at Amsterdam in April 1669. (See 'Comenius in England', p. 26.)

Desmarets' 'Antirrheticus', attacking Comenius, published in summer, 1669.

Komenský's reply, entitled *Continuatio admonitionis fraternae*, published at Amsterdam in the late autumn of 1669.

1670. Comenius died at Amsterdam on 15 November and was buried in the Walloon Church at Naarden.

1681. *Triertium catholicum* published at Amsterdam. *Janua rerum reserata* published at Leiden. (Kvačala, 'Korr. J. A. Komenského', II, No. 133. See 'Comenius in England', p. 49.)

Bibliographies

By ANNA HEYBERGER
Lecturer at Coe College, Cedar Rapids, Iowa
(*Translated from the French by* CORINNE BARHAM)

SELECT BIBLIOGRAPHY OF THE EDUCATIONAL AND SCIENTIFIC WORKS OF COMENIUS

1612–56. *Linguae bohemicae thesaurus, hoc est Lexicon plenissimum, grammatica accurata, idiotismorum elegantiae et emphases adagiaque.* Prepared for press, the manuscript was destroyed in the fire of Leszno in 1656.

1612–56. *Theatrum universitatis rerum,* destroyed in greater part at Leszno in 1656. We possess only the first book, introduced by a pious dedication, two prefaces (one Czech, the other Latin), and a plan of the *Theatrum.* This manuscript fragment, found in 1893, has been published in the 'Veškeré spisy', Vol. I. The original is in the National Museum of Prague.

A copy of a fragment, Part II, Book VII, of the *Amphitheatrum universitatis rerum* was discovered in 1919 and published in the 'Časopis matice moravské', Vol. XLIX, 1925.

1623. The Labyrinth of the World and the Paradise of the Heart. *Labirynt swěta a lusthauz srdce, to gest: swětlé vymalowánj, kterak w tom swětě a wěcech geho wssechněch, nic nenj než matenj a motánj, kolotánj a lopotowánj, mámenj a ssalba, bjda a tesknost, naposledy omrzenj wsseho a zauffánj: Ale kdož doma w srdcy swém sedě, s gediným Pánem Bohem se uzawjrá, ten sám k prawému a plnému mysli upokogenj a radosti že přicházý.* With no indication of place, 1631. In the second edition, Amsterdam, 1663, the author alters the title to *Labirynt swěta a rág srdce.* A number of successive editions followed and the *Labyrinth* has been translated into several languages, even in modern times. There is a French adaptation of it by M. de Crayencourt (Danel, Lille, 1906), taken from the English translation of Count Lützow (London, 1901, 1902 and 1905, in Cambridge University Library), and also a German translation (Jena, 1908). The critical edition, in Czech, is in the 'Veškeré spisy', Vol. XV.

1627–32. Czech Didactic: *Didaktika, to gest uměnj umělého wyučowánj. Kterak by totiž člowěk, dřjw než na těle wzroste a staw swůg začne, wssemi tomu, což ku potřebě a ozdobám přjtomného y budaucýho žiwota přináležj, sstastně, snadně, plně wyučen, a tak potěssené k žiwotu obogjmu nastrogen být mohl.*

The manuscript of the Didactic was discovered by Ev. Purkyně at Leszno in 1841. It now belongs to the National Museum of Prague. First edition, Prague, 1849. Critical edition in the 'Veškeré spisy', Vol. IV.

Didactica Magna, universale omnes omnia docendi artificium exhibens, sive certus et exquisitus modus per omnes alicuius Christiani regni communitates, oppida et vicos tales erigendi scholas, ut omnis utriusque sexus iuventus, nemine usquam neglecto, litteris informari, moribus expoliri, pietate imbui eaque ratione intra pubertatis annos ad omnia, quae praesentis et futurae vitae sunt, instrui possit compendiose, iucunde, solide. Published for the first time in 1657, as a prefix to the *Opera didactica omnia.* A number of editions have been published as complete or abridged translations, in German, English (M. W. Keatinge, London, 1896 and 1910), Italian, Polish, Russian, Slovenian, and Czech.

1628 (?)–31. *Informatorium sskoly mateřské, to gest pořádná a zřetedlná zpráwa, kterak rodičowé pobožnj y samy y skrze chůwy, pěstauny giné pomocnjky swé, negdražssj swůg klenot, djtky swé milé, w prwnjm gegich a počátečnjm wěku rozumné a počestně k sláwě Bohu, sobě ku potěssenj, djtkám pak swým na spasenj wésti a cwiciti magj.* The Czech manuscript, found at Leszno by A. Gindely, is kept in the National Museum of Prague. First edition, Prague, 1858. Critical edition in 'Veškeré spisy', Vol. IV.

Comenius then wrote out the work in German and published it at Leszno in 1633, and at Leipzig in 1634: *Informatorium der Mutterschul*; then in Latin (1653), in the *Opera didactica omnia*, pars I, pp. 198–249: *Schola infantiae sive de provida juventutis primo sexennio educatione.* The work appeared in Polish at Torun, 1636; in English, under the title of *School of infancy*, in London, 1641. In the nineteenth century there were many editions in German and Czech, four in English, five in Russian, one in Croatian, one in Swedish and one in Italian.

1628–31. *Janua linguarum reserata, sive Seminarium linguarum et scientiarum omnium, hoc est, compendiosa latinam (et quamlibet aliam) linguam, una cum scientiarum, artiumque omnium fundamentis, perdiscendi methodus; sub titulis centum, periodis autem mille comprehensa.* Leszno, 1631 (Columbia University Library, New York).

The work was printed in the *Opera didactica omnia*, pars I, pp. 250–302. There were a great number of editions, in twelve European languages and several Oriental ones. The work appeared first in English, edited by a French refugee, John Anchoran, as *Porta Linguarum Trilinguis, The Gate of Tongues Unlocked and opened*, London, 1631, with some doubt as to the authorship, but this was soon corrected. This edition is in the Cambridge University Library. There were several later English editions, e.g. 1638 (in Cambridge University Library); the first in France is dated 1642 (Bibliothèque Nationale).

1632. *Ratio disciplinae ordinisque Fratrum Bohemorum. Recens e bohemico Latina facta.*

1632. *Synopsis historica persecutionum Ecclesiae Bohemicae, jam inde a primordiis conversionis suae, hoc est, anno 894, ad annum usque 1632 continuata. Et nunc primum edita.* Lugduni Batavorum apud Franciscum Moyardum, MDCXLVII. Second edition: *Historia persecutionum Ecclesiae Bohemicae, jam inde a primordiis conversionis suae ad Christianismum, hoc est, anno* 894 *ad annum usque* 1632, *Ferdinando secundo Austriaco regnante, in qua inaudita hactenus Arcana politica, consilia, artes, praesentium bellorum verae causae et judicia horrenda exhibentur.* Nunc primum edita cum duplici Indice. Anno Domini MDCXLVIII (Bibliothèque Nationale).

In Czech: *Hystorya o těžkých protiwenstwjch Cyrkwe české, hned od počátku gegjho na wjru křesť'anskau obrácenj, w létu Páně* 894, *až do léta* 1632, *za panowánj Ferdynanda II. S připogenjm hystorye o persekucy Waldenských roku* 1655 *stalé.* Leszno, 1655. Reprinted: Amsterdam, 1663. Last reprinted: Prague, 1922.

In German: *Kurzer historischer Begriff der Verfolgungen, welche über die böhmische Kirche ergangen* (in Switzerland), 1650. Reprinted under the title *Böhmisches Martyr-büchlein*, Zurich, 1669.

English translation: *History of the Bohemian persecution from the beginning of Christianity in the year* 894 *to the year* 1632, London, 1650. Then there followed numerous editions in Czech, German and Latin. In the preface to the Czech edition of 1655, Comenius mentions a French translation, but we possess no information as to this latter.

1632. *Physicae ad Lumen divinum reformatae Synopsis, Philodidacticorum et Theodidactorum censurae exposita.* Lipsiae, sumptibus Gotofredi Grossi, bibliopolae, anno MDCXXXIII.

Two editions in Amsterdam, 1643 (in Cambridge University Library) and 1645, followed, and then the Paris one 'apud Olivarium de Varennes' in 1647 (Bibliothèque Nationale). There is an English translation: *Naturall Philosophie reformed by Divine light: or a synopsis of Physicks*, London, 1651 (Bibliothèque Nationale and Cambridge University Library). The work was republished once more in 1702, at Halle, by the theologian Joachim Lange. The critical edition came out in the 'Veškeré spisy', Vol. I.

1632. *Astronomia ad lumen physicum reformanda: novis non ad placitum fictis, sed veris et realibus, e coeli natura desumptis, hypothesibus superstruenda.* The manuscript is lost.

1632–33. *Januae linguarum reseratae Vestibulum, quo primus ad Latinam linguam aditus tirunculis paratur*, Leszno, 1633. A number of successive editions followed in various countries. The Paris one, in 1646, *Vestibulum linguae latinae et Dictionarium vestibulare cum interpretatione gallica; itemque Grammatica vestibularis gallice versa*, appeared with a French preface, 'from the publisher to the reader' (Bibliothèque Nationale). The *Opera didactica omnia* (pars I, pp. 301–17) includes the *Januae reseratae Vestibulum*.

In 1678 an illustrated *Vestibulum* was published at Nuremberg, for the teaching of German, Latin and Greek (Cornell University Library, Ithaca, N.Y.).

1634. *Conatuum Comenianorum Praeludia. Porta sapientiae reserata sive Pansophiae Christianae Seminarium. Hoc est nova, compendiosa et solida omnes scientias et artes, et quidquid manifesti vel occulti est, quod ingenio humano penetrare, sollertiae imitari, linguae eloqui datur, brevius, verius, melius, quam hactenus, addiscendi methodus.* Auctore Reverendo Clarissimoque viro, Domino *Johanne Amoso Comenio.* Published without Comenius' knowledge, by Samuel Hartlib, at Oxford, MDCXXXVII. (In the Cambridge University Library.)

In 1639 Hartlib republished the work in London, this time with the author's consent, under the title: *Reverendi et clarissimi viri Johannis Amos Comenii, Pansophiae Prodromus, in quo admirandi illius et vere incomparabilis operis necessitas, possibilitas, utilitas solide, perspicue et eleganter demonstratur.* A preface, written by Hartlib, precedes the text, which is followed by the treatise *Conatuum pansophicorum Dilucidatio* (Bibliothèque Nationale and Cambridge University Library).

Hartlib also published an English translation (made by himself) entitled: *A reformation of schooles designed in two excellent treatises: the first where of summarily sheweth, the great necessity of a generall reformation of common learning. What grounds of hope there are for such a reformation. How it may be brought to passe,* followed by *Dilucidation answering certaine Objections, made against the Endeavours and Means of Reformation in Common Learning, expressed in the foregoing Discourse.* London, MDCXLII (British Museum and Cambridge University Library).

The Leiden Latin edition followed in 1644 (Bibliothèque Nationale and Cambridge University Library). A Paris edition is mentioned by Comenius in a letter to his friend, the editor Montanus (Patera,' Korr.' p. 238), but no copy has been handed down to us. For critical edition, see 'Veškeré spisy', Vol. I.

1637. *De sermonis latini studio, per Vestibulum, Januam, Palatium et Thesauros latinitatis, quadripartito gradu plene absolvendo, Didactica Dissertatio. Cui additur in usum iuventutis formatorum, de editorum iam in lucem Vestibuli et Januae usu debito Informatorium.* Vratislaviae, 1638. Second edition, London, 1639, added to the second edition of the *Pansophiae Prodromus* (in Cambridge University Library); the third appeared at Leiden, 1644 (in Cambridge University Library); the fourth in the *Opera didactica omnia,* pars I. For critical edition see 'Veškeré spisy', Vol. VI.

1638. *Conatuum pansophicorum dilucidatio in gratiam censorum facta.* Published by Hartlib on the occasion of the reprinting of the *Prodromus,* London, MDCXXXIX. Second edition at Leiden in 1649. Third edition in the *Opera didactica omnia,* pars I. The text of the critical edition, in the 'Veškeré spisy' (Vol. I), is a reprint of the London edition.

1640–42. *Janua rerum, sive metaphysica pansophica.* So far as we know Comenius published 5 pages of it at Leszno in 1649 (letter from Nigrin to Hesenthaler, 'Archives of the National Museum of Prague', Ep. Com. XIV), which are lost. In 1661 the author wrote to Montanus 'nunc luci paratur *Janua rerum (quam sapientiam primam et lucem mentium, vulgo, Metaphysicam vocant)*' (Patera, 'Korr.' p. 241). Yet all we now possess is the posthumous work: *Janua rerum reserata, hoc est sapientia prima (quam vulgo Metaphysicam vocant) ita mentibus hominum adaptata, ut per eam in totum rerum ambitum, omnemque interiorem rerum ordinem, et in omnes intimas rebus coaeternas veritates prospectus pateat catholicus: simulque ut eadem omnium humanarum cogitationum, sermonum, operum, fons et scaturigo, formaque ac norma esse appareat.* Leiden, 1681 (Library of Prague National Museum).

1641. *Abrahamus Patriarcha. Scena repraesentatus.* Anno 1641 in Januario, sub examen Scholae publicum. Printed at Amsterdam in 1661 (Bibliothèque Nationale). A school play.

1641. *Via lucis, vestigata et vestiganda, hoc est rationabilis disquisitio, quibus modis intellectualis animorum Lux, Sapientia, per omnes omnium hominum mentes, et gentes, jam tandem sub mundi vesperam feliciter spargi possit. Libellus ante annos viginti sex in Anglia scriptus, nunc demum typis exscriptus et in Angliam remissus.* Amsterdam, 1668. The work opens with a dedication to the Royal Society, composed in April 1668 (Bibliothèque Nationale). English translation by E. T. Campagnac, Liverpool, 1938.

1641. *Pansophiae diatyposis ichnographica et orthographica delineatione totius futuri operis amplitudinem, dimensionem, usus, adumbrans.* Danzig, 1643, and Amsterdam, 1645 (Bibliothèque Nationale and Cambridge University Library). In English: *An Orthographical delineation, or true draught of the pansophicall temple etc.* translated by Jeremy Collier. London, 1651 (in Cambridge University Library).

1643–47. *Linguarum methodus novissima, fundamentis didacticis solide superstructa, latinae linguae exemplo realiter demonstrata, scholarum usibus iam tandem examussim accommodata, sed et insuper aliis studiorum generibus magno usu accommodanda. Ante tamen eruditorum judicio publice exposita, seriisque ac severis censuris submissa.* Published at Leszno, MDCXLVIII–IX. Second edition in the *Opera didactica omnia*, pars II. Critical edition, 'Veškeré spisy', Vol. VI.

1644–45. *De rerum humanarum emendatione consultatio catholica, ad genus humanum, ante alios vero ad Eruditos, Religiosos, Potentes, Europae.*

Two parts: (*a*) the *Panegersia, excitatorium universale*, and (*b*) the *Panaugia, ubi, de accendenda mentibus ante omnia Luce quadam universali, in qua Omnes, Omnia, Omnino videre possint, consultatur*, came out anonymously and in very limited issue, at Amsterdam, in 1666. One of the two existing copies of these two parts is in Prague University Library.

Without knowledge of the first edition, Buddeus had the *Panegersia* published from the manuscript, at Halle, in 1702 (Bibliothèque Nationale and Cambridge University Library).

We do not know whether the other parts, which Nigrin edited from the material left by Comenius, ever saw the light of day.

1651. *Schola pansophica, hoc est, universalis sapientiae officina, ab annis aliquot ubiubigentium erigi optata: nunc autem auspiciis illustrissimi domini D. Sigismundi Racoci de Felseovadas, etc., Saros-Pataki Hungarorum feliciter erigenda, anno redditae mundo salutis* MDCLI. Second edition: *Opera didactica omnia*, pars III, pp. 6–60.

1651. *Primitiae laborum scholasticorum in illustri Patakino gymnasio in majus et melius transformari coepto:* 1. *De Cultura Ingeniorum oratio, habita in Scholae Patakinae auditorio majori* 24 *Novembr. Anno* MDCL, *a Johanne Amoso Comenio, Hunno Brodensi Moravo.* 2. *De primario ingenia colendi instrumento, solerter versando, libris, oratio. Sub laborum auspicia in Patakinae scholae auditorio majori recitata, anno* MDCL. 28 *Novembr. Opera didactica omnia*, pars III, pp. 71–114.

1651. *Eruditionis scholasticae pars prima, Vestibulum, rerum et linguarum fundamenta exhibens*, Sáros-patak, 1651–52. The cycle opens with a dedication to the master Stephen Tolnai. There follow: (*a*) the *Vestibulum linguarum*; (*b*) the *Rudimenta grammaticae*; (*c*) the *Repertorium vestibulare, sive lexici latini rudimentum*; (*d*) *de Instituendis e latinae linguae Vestibulo exercitiis ad praeceptorem commonefactio.* Published in the *Opera didactica omnia*, pars III. The work had previously appeared at Sáros-patak in 1650–51, but no copy of this original edition seems to have survived.

1651. *Eruditionis scholasticae*, pars II. *Janua, rerum et linguarum structuram externam exhibens.* Comprises a preface dedicated to the master Paul Kapossius, and following that:

(*a*) *Sylva latinae linguae, vocum derivatarum copiam explicans, sive Lexicon januale.*

(*b*) *Grammatica janualis, continens residuum grammaticae vestibularis.*

(*c*) *Janualis rerum et verborum contextus, historiolam rerum continens.*

The work stands in this form in the *Opera didactica omnia*, pars III. It had been published previously at Sáros-patak in 1652.

1651. *Eruditionis scholasticae*, pars III. *Atrium, rerum et linguarum ornamenta exhibens*, Sáros-patak, 1651; Nuremberg, at Endterus', 1655 (in Cambridge University Library); and finally *Opera didactica omnia*, pars III; comprises a dedication to the master Johannes Etzedius, the *Ars ornatoria sive grammatica elegans*, the *Latinae linguae Atrium, rerum historiam elegantiori exornatam stylo exhibens.* The *Atrium* appeared 'in usum scholae Patakinae', in 1652, and was republished in the *Opera didactica omnia*, pars III. The *Ars ornatoria* appeared again at London, 1664 (in Cambridge University Library).

The *Lexicon atriale Latino-Latinum, simplices et nativas rerum nomenclationes e Januae linguae jam notas, in elegantes varie commutare docens* was published only at Amsterdam, in 1657 (Bibliothèque Nationale and Cambridge University Library).

1652. *Laborum scholasticorum in illustri Patakino gymnasio continuatio.* This selection contains a dedication to Andrew of Klobusić, and three dissertations: 1. *Methodi verae encomia. Ex fabula de Labyrintho Daedaleo, filoque Ariadnes. Patakini habita sub tempus erigendae classis latinae primae, quae Vestibularis est.* Anno 1651, Febr. 13; 2. *De utilitate accuratae rerum nomenclaturae oratiuncula, recitata sub tempus erigendae classis secundae, Janualis,* 14 Martii; 3. *De eleganti elegantiarum studio, oratiuncula, habita sub tempus erectionis classis latinae tertiae, Atrialis seu Rhetoricae, in illustri schola Patakina,* anno MDCLII, Jan. 10.

These treatises were published at Sáros-patak in 1652; later in the *Opera didactica omnia,* pars III, pp. 736–57, and in the 'Veškeré spisy', Vol. IX.

1654. *Orbis sensualium pictus. Hoc est, omnium fundamentalium in mundo rerum et in vita actionum Pictura et Nomenclatura. Die sichtbare Welt, das ist, aller vornehmsten Welt-Dinge und Lebens-Verrichtungen Vorbildung und Benahmung.* Norimbergae, Typis et Sumptibus Michaelis Endteri, anno Salutis MDCLVIII (Bibliothèque Nationale). The *Orbis pictus* opens with a very important preface to the reader. The second edition came out at Nuremberg in 1659, followed by the editions of 1662, 1663, 1664 (in Cambridge University Library), 1666, etc. The English edition bears, in addition to the Latin title, the following English title: *Joh. Amos Comenius's Visible World: or a Picture and Nomenclature of all the chief things that are in the World; and of Men's Employments therein. A Work newly written by the Author in Latine and High-Dutch (being one of his best Essays and the most suitable to children's capacities of any that he hath hitherto made) and translated into English by Charles Hoole, M.A. for the use of Young Latin scholars.* London, MDCLIX (British Museum). Later published: London, 1664 (in British Museum), 1672, 1705, 1727, 1728, 1777 (in Cambridge University Library), etc. Translated into most European languages (bilinguis, trilinguis, quadrilinguis). Of all Comenius' works, this *Orbis Pictus* is, with the exception of the *Janua linguarum,* the one which has been the most often republished up to the present times.

1654. *Schola ludus seu encyclopaedia viva. Hoc est Janua linguarum praxis comica. Res omnes nomenclatura vestitas et vestiendas sensibus ad vivum repraesentandi artificium exhibens amoenum.* Published at Sáros-patak in 1656, with a dedication (dated 24 April 1654); then reprinted in 1657, at Amsterdam, with a new preface (in Cambridge University Library). It was republished in the *Opera didactica omnia,* pars III, where the author makes a change in the title, the expression 'comica' becoming 'scenica'. In 1659 the *Schola ludus* came out at Frankfort with the German translation.

The 'Veškeré spisy' (Vol. IX) gives a critical edition of it.

1657. *Opera didactica omnia. Variis hucusque occasionibus scripta, diversisque locis edita: nunc autem non tantum in unum, ut simul sint, collecta, sed et ultimo conatu in Systema unum mechanice constructum, redacta.* Amstelodami, MDCLVII. Impensis D. Laurentii de Geer.

The work is divided into four parts and opens with a dedicatory epistle to the town of Amsterdam, which is followed by a preface: *Lectoribus piis et prudentibus.* Part I comprises the didactic works composed from 1627 to 1642; Part II those from 1642 to 1650; Part III those from 1650 to 1654; Part IV contains a collection of treatises written in Amsterdam.

1. *Vita gyrus: sive de occasionum varietate.* 2. *Parvulis parvulus omnibus omnia: hoc est, Vestibuli latinae linguae Auctarium.* *Voces latinas primitivas construi coeptas et in sententiolas breves redactas exhibens.* *In praeludium sylvam latinam ingressuris datum.* 3. *Pro latinitate Januae linguarum suae, illiusque praxeos comicae, Apologia.* 4. *Ventilabrum sapientiae, sive, sapienter sua retractandi ars.* 5. *E scholasticis labyrinthis exitus in planum.* 6. *Latium redivivum.* 7. *Typographeum vivum.* 8. *Paradisus juventuti christianae reducendus.* 9. *Traditio lampadis.* (The *Opera didactica omnia* is in the Bibliothèque Nationale and in the Educational Museum of Paris and in the Cambridge University Library.) German translation by J. Reber, Giessen, 1896.

1659. *Cartesius cum sua naturali Philosophia a Mechanicis eversus,* Amsterdami, apud Petrum Montanum MDCLIX (Library of St John's Church, Leszno).

1661 (?). *Sapientiae primae usus Triertium catholicum appellandus, hoc est, humanarum Cogitationum, Sermonum, Operum, Scientiam, Artem, Usum, aperiens Clavis Triuna: sive amabile Logicae, Grammaticae, Pragmaticaeque cum Metaphysica Osculum.*

Mentioned in a letter from Comenius to Montanus (Patera, 'Korr.' p. 241), the work must have been completed by Comenius. The dedication 'Nobilissimis, Magnificis, Amplissimis Amstelodamensis Reipub. D. D. Consulibus' dates back to the year 1670: 'Quatuordecim abierunt anni meae apud Vos hospitationis', the year of the author's death. The *Triertium Catholicum,* however, was only published as a posthumous work at Leiden, in 1681, by the care of Christian V. Nigrin. The only copy is preserved in the library of the Strahov Monastery in Prague. The work has been reproduced in facsimile by the publisher J. Štenc, Prague, 1920.

1667. *Angelus pacis ad Legatos pacis Anglos et Belgas Bredam missus. Indeque ad omnes Christianos per Europam, et mox ad omnes populos per orbem totum mittendus. Ut se sistant, belligerare desistant, pacisque principi, Christo, pacem gentibus jam loquuturo, locum faciant.* Anno MDCLXVII, Mense Maio.

The only known copy of this work is kept in the Provincial Museum (Zemské Museum) at Brno in Moravia.

1668. *Via lucis...* see 1641.

1669. *De Zelo sine scientia et charitate, Admonitio fraterna J. A. Comenii ad D. Samuelem Maresium: Pro minuendis odiis et ampliandis favoribus.* Amstelodami, apud Johannem Jansonium, anno MDCLXIX. There are only three known copies: the one in the Weimar Library, that in the National Library of Vienna, and that in the Archives of the Massachusetts Historical Society, Boston.

1669–70. *Continuatio admonitionis fraternae de temperando charitate zelo. Cum fideli Dehortatione a Pantherina Indole a Larvis, Joh. Comenii ad S.*

Maresium: Pro intentione prima, minuendorum Odiorum ampliandorumque favorum: Aut ad trahendum finaliter obstinatos Divino et humano judicio. Amsterdami, apud Johannem van Someren, Bibliopolam, 1669. The only copy of this work, from which the first thirty-eight paragraphs and the end are missing (it was probably never finished) is to be found in the Public Library at Leningrad. ? *Spicilegium didacticum, artium discendi ac docendi summam brevibus praeceptis exhibens,* J. A. Comenio, collectum et editum a C. V. N. (Christian V. Nigrin), Amstelodami, 1680. Reprinted by J. Kvačala in the 'Korr.' ɪɪ, pp. 303–28.

SELECT BIBLIOGRAPHY OF PUBLICATIONS CONCERNING COMENIUS (IN CHRONOLOGICAL ORDER)

JOHN GAUDEN. 'The love of truth and peace. A sermon preached before the Honourable House of Commons assembled in Parliament.' London, 1641, pp. 41–3. (British Museum Library.)

BAYLE. 'Dictionnaire historique et critique', 1699. An article 'Comenius' (based on the antagonistic writings of Comenius' opponents).

JOH. GOTTFRIED HERDER. 'Ueber den menschenfreundlichen Comenius', in 'Briefe zur Beförderung der Humanität'. Riga, 1795.

KARL VON RAUMER. 'Geschichte der Pädagogik.' Stuttgart, 1843, pp. 46–97. Special edition, 'Johann Amos Comenius', Gutersloh, 1892.

DANIEL BENHAM. 'A sketch of the life of Comenius', preceding the translation of *Informatorium sskoly mateřské; School of infancy.* London, 1858.

ROBERT HERBERT QUICK. 'Essays on educational reformers', 1868 and 1890, English and American editions. Editions in 1899 and 1903, by Appleton & Co., New York, Chapter x: 'Comenius'.

FR. J. ZOUBEK. 'Joh. Amos Comenius, Eine biographische Skizze.' Leipzig, 1871.

DAVID MASSON. 'The Life of John Milton in connection with the Political, Ecclesiastical, and Literary History of his time.' Macmillan & Co. 1873 and 1896 (in the 1896 edition, for reference to Comenius see Vol. ɪɪɪ, pp. 198–215, 220–28, 232–5, 237–9, 661–2, Vol. vɪ, p. 394).

FRANCK. 'Dictionnaire philosophique.' Paris, 1875, Vol. v, an article 'Comenius'.

S. S. LAURIE. 'John Amos Comenius, Bishop of the Moravians, His life and educational works.' London, 1881; Cambridge, 1884, 1887, 1899, 1904; Boston, Mass., 1885; Syracuse, 1892; London, 1899.

J. Kvačala. 'Comenius und Baco.' 1888.

Nicholas Murray Butler. 'The place of Comenius in the history of Education.' Bardeen, Syracuse, N.Y. 1892.

Will S. Monroe. 'Comenius, the Evangelist of Modern Pedagogy.' Boston, 1892.

L. Keller. 'Comenius und die Akademien d. Naturphilosophen des 17. Jahrhunderts.' Berlin, 1895.

M. W. Keatinge. See the *Great Didactic* in the foregoing bibliography, 1896.

Will S. Monroe. 'Comenius and the Beginnings of Educational Reform.' The Great Educators, London, 1900; New York, 1900, 1907.

Ernest Denis. 'La Bohême depuis la Montagne Blanche.' Paris, 1903, pp. 219–33. Czech translation by J. Vančura, Prague, 1921, pp. 268–86, and commentary, pp. 312–25.

Joh. Kvačala. 'Die pädagogische Reform des Comenius in Deutschland bis zum Ausgange des xvii. Jahrhunderts.' Two volumes, Berlin, 1903 and 1904, in the 'Monumenta Germaniae paedagogica'.

L. W. Adamson. 'Pioneers of Modern Education.' London, 1905, Chapters iii–v.

J. Kvačala. 'J. A. Comenius.' Berlin, 1914. Lehmann's series: 'Die grossen Erzieher. Ihre Persönlichkeit und ihre Systeme.'

Robert R. Rusk. 'The doctrines of the great educators.' Macmillan & Co. 1918, Chapter v: 'Comenius.'

Albert Matthews. 'Comenius and Harvard College.' Publications of the Colonial Society of Massachusetts, Vol. xxi, Cambridge, Mass. Special issue, The University Press, 1919.

G. H. Turnbull. 'Samuel Hartlib. A sketch of his life and his relations to J. A. Comenius.' Oxford University Press, 1920.

F. Eckstein. 'Comenius und die Böhmischen Brüder.' Leipzig, 1922.

J. Jakubec. 'Jan Amos Comenius' (with foreword by T. G. Masaryk). Prague, 1928.

R. Fitzgibbon Young. 'Comenius and the Indians of New England', London, 1929; 'Comenius in England', Oxford, 1932; article on Komenský in *Enciclopedia Italiana*, Vol. 20, pp. 248–250.

A. Heyberger. 'Jean Amos Comenius, Sa vie et son œuvre d'éducateur.' Paris, 1930.

C. J. Wright. 'Comenius and the Church Universal.' Barber, London, 1941.

Printed in the United States
By Bookmasters